2004 PO

ONCE UPON A RHYME

IMAGINATION FOR
A NEW GENERATION

GW01319679

Northern Surrey Vol II
Edited by Claire Tupholme

 Young**Writers**

First published in Great Britain in 2004 by:
Young Writers
Remus House
Coltsfoot Drive
Peterborough
PE2 9JX
Telephone: 01733 890066
Website: www.youngwriters.co.uk

SB ISBN 1 84460 602 3

Foreword

Young Writers was established in 1991 and has been passionately devoted to the promotion of reading and writing in children and young adults ever since. The quest continues today. Young Writers remains as committed to engendering the fostering of burgeoning poetic and literary talent as ever.

This year's Young Writers competition has proven as vibrant and dynamic as ever and we are delighted to present a showcase of the best poetry from across the UK. Each poem has been carefully selected from a wealth of *Once Upon A Rhyme* entries before ultimately being published in this, our twelfth primary school poetry series.

Once again, we have been supremely impressed by the overall high quality of the entries we have received. The imagination, energy and creativity which has gone into each young writer's entry made choosing the best poems a challenging and often difficult but ultimately hugely rewarding task - the general high standard of the work submitted amply vindicating this opportunity to bring their poetry to a larger appreciative audience.

We sincerely hope you are pleased with our final selection and that you will enjoy *Once Upon A Rhyme Northern Surrey Vol II* for many years to come.

Contents

Luke Boyd (11)   48
Robyn Davies (10)   48

Educare Small School
Toby Lawson (9)   49
Lily Yorke (10)   49
Hannah Oxford (7)   50
Dion Allen (8)   50
Harrison Parker (8)   51
Liberty Blackmore (11)   51
Pablo Linares-Bowles (11)   52
Ollie Summers (8)   52

Latchmere Junior School
Lara Hyson (9)   52
Sarah Stacey (9)   53
Holly Milner (9)   53
Gemma Annetts (8)   54
Taylor Edgington (9)   54
Patrick McCarthy (8)   55
Erna Starr (9)   55
Emilia Jagiello (9)   56
Ashna Gupta (10)   57
Isabella Lindsley (9)   58
Luke Geraghty (9)   59
Charlie Flowers (9)   60
Kirsten Guest (8)   61
Ross Morey (9)   62
Daniel Meegan (8)   63
Leonie Maier (10)   64
Holly Clemens (10)   64
Farah Malik (10)   65
Rosanna Quigley (11)   65
Rachel Shannon (11)   66
Michaela Betts (10)   67
Gemma Downs (10)   68
Gregory Winter (10)   68
Thomas Hearn (9)   69
Gareth Dean (9)   69
William Conder (10)   70
Nick Wood (10)   71

Katherine McLoughlin (8)	72
Sarah Howden (9)	72
Samuel Kopinski (9)	73
Charlotte Seers (9)	73
Isabel Evans (8)	74
Lucy Mahoney (8)	74
Robert Hayes (8)	74
George Faulkner (8)	75
Nadir Adoul-Rutherfoord (9)	75

St Joseph's RC School, Epsom

Louis Ekoku (8)	75
Luke Haynes (8)	76
Nicole Nartallo (8)	76
Giulietta Tallo (9)	76
Conor Bracken (9)	77
Niamh Donnelly (8)	77
Daniel Diaz (9)	77
Teresa O'Leary (9)	78
Dominic Roche (9)	78
John Twells (9)	78
Laura Cooke (9)	79
James Hampshire (9)	79
Conor Davison (8)	79
Daniel Schifano (9)	80
Andrew Doyle (9)	80
Olivia Leitch (9)	80
Caitlin Rosbotham (8)	81
Drew O'Hare (9)	81
Johnny Ciesco (8)	81
Fiona Hampshire (9)	82
Elizabeth Dawe (9)	82
Katie-Jane Hinksman (9)	82
Mario Raffa (9)	83
Grace McGovern (9)	83
Charlotte Cane (9)	83
Charlie Gregory (9)	84

St Mary's RC Junior School, Carshalton

Beth Smallwood (8)	84
Sabina Wantoch (10)	85

Emily Godfrey (9)	109
Sian Gray (10)	109
Fiona Horrod (10)	110
Danielle Wilson (10)	110
Natalie Hooper (10)	111
Eman Omer (9)	111
Jack Montague (10)	112
Rachel Bradford (9)	112
Tjasha Stroud (10)	113
Josh Corrigan (10)	113

Woodside Junior School

Daniel Goudie (10)	113
Naomi Harrison (10)	114
Shenaid Tapper (10)	114
Jodie Micallef (9)	115
William Dunne	115
Bakhitah Bundu-Kamara (10)	115
Sheldon Kyme (9)	116
Amy Lackenby (8)	116
Geoffrey Whitby (10)	116
Tajay Ashmeade (10)	117
Jamie Lowe (9)	117
Kelly Henry (9)	117
Lauren Carr (9)	118
Janaki Srikanthan (9)	118
Charlotte Devenish (9)	119
Seraish Edwards (9)	120
Jessica Kidd	120
Jodie McQuade (9)	120
Nikki Mikellides (8)	121
Eden Reeves Lamb	121
Daniel Clayton (8)	121
Charley Pilbro	122
Crystal Medcalf	122
Melad Ali	123
Sachadena Walker (9)	123
Molly Algar	124
William Howells (8)	124
Asim Qureshi (8)	124
Michael Vernon (9)	125

The Poems

Nightmare

I strolled out into the starry night,
I heard howls and wails that gave me such a fright,
Although the glistening moon and lamp posts still shone bright,
The beauty and peace made me think *what a wonderful sight.*

Suddenly sharp shivers ran down my spine,
There was a massive flash and I knew this was a sign,
I heard cats purr and shabby dogs whine
And I saw old-fashioned ghosts all in a long ghastly line.

I found myself falling, falling deep into the ground,
The wind rushing and screeching down my ears
Made a horrible sound,
My back banged hard on the wooden floor.

So I landed in a great big mound,
My head made me feel like I was quickly spinning round and round,
I walked down a dark alleyway,
I felt like I was being whizzed away,
Then I turn down a tunnel and see the living day,
I wake up and my nightmare is quickly over!

Charlotte Haime (10)
Barrow Hedges Primary School

Slug

A slug crawls carefully across the ground
Where it crawls, a silver trail will be found
As it moves cautiously across
A dark shadow is cast over it
A foot comes down and it goes
Squash!

Daniel Hunt (10)
Barrow Hedges Primary School

About My Brother's Life

He started off with a heart murmur
Then when he was 8 years old
Great Ormond Street found a problem with his bowel
Why did it take so long?
Why? Why? Why?
Now he's got a stoma bag
And a feeding tube.
I am happy when I see him.

Happy and relaxed,
Running in sports day,
Dancing at a disco,
Getting on with his life,
I am happy,
I am happy,
But he is handicapped,
But he is handicapped.

Grant Fulker (10)
Barrow Hedges Primary School

My Hamster Ate A Firework!

My hamster ate a firework and zoomed off into space,
His nose blew up humungous and dropped right off his face,
His eyes went all googly and nearly popped out of their sockets,
He was standing on the moon and saw some stray rockets,
The next day I went to see him,
I saw a hamster not at all thin but fat, fat, fat,
As fat as Postman Pat's cat,
I heard 10 beeps and a crash,
Next time I'll feed him hamster mash.

Poppy Radford (10)
Barrow Hedges Primary School

Midnight

In the rainforest on a very hot day,
Midnight, the panther was catching her prey
After that she went to explore!

She went into the rainforest more and more,
She saw amazing things like red tree frogs
And mansion toads, also she saw woolly monkeys
And howler monkeys, which howl,
Let me describe them to you,
Somehow they have got big owl eyes.

Midnight slept for a while for she was tired,
Midnight woke up in the morning
And all of a sudden started yawning.

Midnight went into the rainforest deeper and deeper,
Midnight came across a parrot called Mr Money
Who was eating honey and looked funny,
So the panther said, 'Would you like to be my friend?'
Mr Money said, 'Yes, I do, I've always wanted a friend like you.'
'Me too!' said Midnight.

So the panther and parrot have a friend,
Now that's . . . *the end!*

Molly Jepp (9)
Barrow Hedges Primary School

Dogs

Little white fluffy paws,
A little squishy nose,
Little sharp pearl-white teeth,
Tiny pudgy toes.

Olivia Johnston (9)
Barrow Hedges Primary School

My Mum

My mum
Has a rather big bum
And a rather big tum,
She's very proud,
But very loud,
She has a very good brain,
But is a bit insane,
Well, that's my mum,
With the rather big bum.

Emma Witcomb (10)
Barrow Hedges Primary School

My Cat, Tigger

My cat Tigger has a very fluffy tail
He shakes it and curls it
And chases it round and round
So when his play time is over
He creeps in through his flap
To lay on the carpet asleep on his back.

Emma Howard (9)
Barrow Hedges Primary School

Darkness Poem

Darkness is fun, darkness is great,
Foxes playing in the middle of the night,
Bats flying, foxes eating, rabbits hopping,
Darkness can be scary too,
With noises we can't recognise,
Suddenly a person jumps out and says, 'Boo.'

Daniel Wilding (10)
Barrow Hedges Primary School

Food Fight

Yes! It's lunchtime! Whoopee!
Off to the lunch room!
Food swaps, food fights every day,
To the heavenly food lagoon!

I look in my lunchbox
And there I see,
Healthy stuff
Looking up at me!

Yuck! Muesli,
Sandwiches,
These should be
A hit with Liz.

Lunchtime is over
But now guess what?
I had the unhealthiest
Lunch of the lot!

Clare Woodroffe (10)
Barrow Hedges Primary School

The Heart Of A Fire!

A tiny flicker sparks to life;
the flicker grows and laps the wood,
paper shrivels as the flame moves slowly,
smothering everything it touches. It eats its way
relentlessly upward,
engulfing all in its path.
Wood begins to crumble,
collapsing in a shower of sparks,
leaving steady orange and blue tongues,
eating around the coal
and the glow deepens in the heart.

Matthew Manfield (10)
Cleves School

Eye Over Africa

In the plains of Kenya
All is calm,
The only sound is the wind,
Gazelles are frolicking
In the grass,
The lions sleep in peace,
Yes, the lions sleep in peace.

In the desert,
The ground is dry
And people die of thirst,
But life continues,
From the winding snake,
To the cacti standing tall,
Yes, the cacti standing tall.

In the mighty jungle,
Monkeys leap
From tree to branch to vine,
The chimps all screech,
Gorillas grunt
And all life flourishes,
Yes, all life flourishes.

You can see it and hear it,
But never deny it,
The beauty that is Africa,
Yes, the beauty that is Africa.

Joe Finney
Cleves School

Sunny

S hines throughout the day when the creatures run free
U ntil the night falls and owls hoot
N ever does the sun bring a frown
N ever does it bring a tear
Y ou will always know the sun is here.

Kim Dawkins (11)
Cleves School

The Simpsons

T he Simpsons is my favourite programme
H omer is in The Simpsons as a character
E very episode brings out a laugh

S adly they only go on for half an hour but they are
always on tomorrow
I have two of The Simpsons games on PS2
M e and my brother sit down and watch them every night
P eople in The Simpsons have a yellow skin colour
S unday there are new Simpsons so we rush to the sofa
to get the best seat and then sit down and watch them
O n Sky One The Simpsons are on but not on BBC2
N o we haven't missed one episode in my little life
S chool is OK when you go home to play on The Simpsons
but when the real thing's on you rush to the TV and
never play it again (until tomorrow).

Jamie Bartlett (11)
Cleves School

Spring

The trees are waking from their sleep,
The sun is brighter than before,
The bluebells hang their heads and weep,
The grass is sparkling white no more.

The fields are filling up with sheep,
Flowers are opening their heads,
The little lambs now bleat and leap,
As mothers call them from their beds.

The season, spring, has just begun,
Lots of new leaves are on the trees,
Now we can play out in the sun,
Smell fragrant blossom on the breeze.

Louise Leitch (10)
Cleves School

The Fairy Ball

Once upon a time, a girl named Mary,
Whilst walking the woods met a fairy,
The fairy had a fright
And flew into the night.

Mary thought it was a dream,
So ran and ran till she met the stream,
She tumbled and stumbled into the water,
Then the fairy appeared and caught her.

Fairy told Mary about the fairy ball,
Which was taking place in the fairy hall,
The fairy invited her to come
And that she could not tell her mum.

Mary got into her lovely dress
And tried not to get it into a mess,
Where they danced all night long,
Till the clock went dong.

Alice Cheeseman (11)
Cleves School

The Sea

It is a horrible, miserable day,
The sea is crashing on the shore,
The waves are like a gigantic mouth,
The different sized footprints are vanishing in the sand,
Nobody is on the beach to play,
It is as if a giant hand has picked them up
And taken them all away,
There is a huge, strong current
And the sea is quite grey,
It sounds very angry, just like a roaring lion.

Alexandra Laven (10)
Cleves School

I Wish, I Wish I Was A Dog

I wish, I wish I was a dog
I'd sleep all day and night
I'd run around the woods like mad
And give the birds a fright.

I wish, I wish I was a dog
I'd wag my tail with glee
I'd wait until my mum came home
And smile at her happily.

I wish, I wish I was a dog
I wish I was a Lab
I'd stare at my fur coat all day
And think that it was fab!

I wish, I wish I was a dog
I'd love to go for walks
The only problem that I'd have
Is that I cannot talk!

I wish, I wish I was a dog
I'd live in a nice home
I'd look forward to Sundays
Because I'd get a bone!

Rebecca Knapp (11)
Cleves School

Kittens

I love kittens at night
I love the way they play fight
A kitten with a mouse to chase
Is beautiful and full of grace
A kitten climbing up something
Is such an adorable little thing
I love their amber, blue or green eyes
I know a kitten has no lies.

Shireene Kalbassi (10)
Cleves School

Human Zoo

Rush, rush, rush! What's on today?
Is it burgers, is it sausages?
They bought it . . . fried it . . . served it!
Floor smells of polish, the food is baking.

We grab a tray, grab a plate,
Then we line up with our mate.
We grab a knife, a spoon and fork,
Table and a seat, remembering a glass of drink.

Dinner lady said to me,
Hurry up it's time to flee,
Have some meat or something sweet,
Chop-chop girl or I'll just pick.

Some go mad for fish and chips
Or nuggets with dripping dips.
Grilled sausages aren't for me,
Fat, skinny, mini or maxi pizza is the pick!

Pudding's next, a crazy rush for
Table full of cake and more,
The dinner lady said snacks are trash,
But I had seen her scoff some crisps, off duty!

I swear, I saw her eating it,
Made me blink and have a fit.
I was mad, mad as can be,
In the serving hatch, was where it took place.

Edie eats and talks with jaw ajar,
Adam chews like a racing car,
Danny dribbles, Nelly just nibbles,
Lunch from one 'til two becomes a feeding frenzy,
At our school down in the dining hall.

What are you having for today?

Natasha Cheung (11)
Cleves School

The Alligator

Basking lazily in the summer warmth of May,
But watching his river throughout the day,
No animal ever strays near,
Because down his throat they would disappear.

He descends down to the river for some food,
Confident and in a good mood,
To the other side of the river he is bound,
He departs from the bank without a sound.

On the opposite bank, nearly dry,
He chose the animal that would die,
A young deer would be his prey,
To keep him fed till another day.

The alligator pounced, jaws open wide,
The startled animal had nowhere to hide,
The deer suffered no pain,
Lord of the river fed again!

James Pepper (10)
Cleves School

The Trampoline

I like to go on a trampoline
Up to the sky so blue
Oh I do think it is the nicest thing
Anyone can do!

Bouncing high and over the wall
Till I can see so much
Houses, gardens and trees
All over the land that I can see

Till I look down on the garden green
Down on the bouncy mat below
Up in the air I go flying again
Up in the air and down!

Craig Humphrey (10)
Cleves School

My Own Secret Fairy

My own secret fairy is pretty and small
She dances around all day
She's not one of Mary Barker's fairies but
She's mine and comes out in May
Her name is Twinkle, she's very helpful
Twinkle has tiny little dancing shoes
So when I am at my ballet classes
Twinkle goes up on her toes too
She's very quiet, does not make a noise
And wears a pretty pink dress with
Delicate white roses which sit on her dress
Like falling snowflakes at twilight
And later on she sings at night
A short and sweet little song -
O how I float and flutter and dance
I come and help you too, so keep on your toes
And dance around and tomorrow you do and do.

Lydia Chitnis (11)
Cleves School

What Is The Moon?

Is the moon always bright or is it sometimes midnight black?
Is it slower than a turtle or could it beat you round a track?
Is it heavier than hippos or could you lift it on your back?
Is it bigger than the Earth or does it fit in Santa's sack?

Does the moon ever change its shape or is it always like a ball?
Does it ever grow in size or is it always nice and small?
Is it ever really cold, does it need to wear a shawl?
Was the moon ever a baby, did it ever crawl?

Does the moon have an entrance, does it have a door?
Are there any rules over there, does it abide by the law?
Does it own any wealth or is it very, very poor?
Does it have a centre, just like an apple core?

Sophie Chapman (11)
Cleves School

Dragon

It's a fire-breathing menace,
When it's soaring through the sky.
Jets of flame from its mouth,
Let the humans die.

Its angry eyes are burning,
In hatred and malice,
It's flying round in circles,
Burning down the palace.

When it's sleeping calm and still,
The humans come to kill,
The dragon in his cave,
A monster in its sleep.

He awakens with a roar,
A flame comes burning through,
His castle door destroyed,
He stands up waiting.

As the humans come,
With swords and arrows,
Piercing his chest,
He falls down in eternal rest.

Jake Freestone (11)
Cleves School

Dreams

D reamcatchers twinkle over our beds in the moonlight,
R emembering people and places we have been,
E yelids closing as darkness falls,
A ction replays revolving in our minds,
M ore fantasies to fuel our weary minds,
S urrounded by images floating through our heads.

Lucy Hawkes (11)
Cleves School

Feelings

P ain is like dark
A ngry and sinister
I n the blood it stirs
N othing is quite like it

H appiness is a great feeling
A feeling that makes you smile
P arties make happiness come alive
P erhaps it should be celebrated
Y ou and I know that happiness lasts forever

A nger is what hides in the dark
N othing can stop it coming
G reater it grows inside
R apidly it bursts out
Y ou don't mean it when it happens.

Lucy Dinnage (10)
Cleves School

Mars

We are going to Mars
Escaping in our red cars
And passing the shiny stars
Reversing with the boosts
Ejecting in our spacesuits
Gathering speed to Mars
Observing for any life
Inspecting crashed rockets
Not taking any risks
Getting ready for lift-off
Thrusting off into space
Ordering the spacecrafts
Mission to Mars is over
Approaching the planet Earth
Resembling rocket orbits
Seeing the people again
We are going to Mars!

James King (11)
Cleves School

The Vanishing Act

She was nothing
  Just a solitary candle
    Flickering in the wind
      Silent as the night.

Walking down a moonlit path
  She stumbles on the earth
    She longed to be a bird
      And fly away from her troubles.

She walked across the rocks
  As the waves broke against the cliffs
    She swooped down into the sea
      A dolphin in the ocean.

She was alone
  Just a lonely soul
    And as she lived longing for a friend
      She slowly began to fade.

She faded from memory
  She faded from all thought
    And as she glided into the night
      She vanished . . .

Emily Winchester (11)
Cleves School

Colours

Red is the blood running round your body,
Black is the darkness of the night which fills the Earth,
Yellow is the sun brightening the sky,
Pink is the softness of a mother's touch,
Green is the colour which fills the grass,
Blue is the sea, sky and anger,
White is the peace of the Earth and Heaven,
But every colour, shade and feeling fills our hearts with warmth.

Emily Brown (11)
Cleves School

I'm A Cowgirl

Yeehah, I'm rockin' and a rollin' down the street
I'm lookin' kinda busy but I'm still on my feet
Trippin' and troopin' tired buckarooin'
That's what makes me . . . me

What's . . . what? Who's . . . who?
I'm from Texas and that's the truth
You don't believe me, well you're wrong
I'm a cowgirl and that's the meanin' of this song

Yeehah, I'm rocking' and a rollin' down the street
I'm lookin' kinda busy but I'm still on my feet
Trippin' and troopin' tired buckarooin'
That's what makes me . . . me

Where's . . . this? I'm . . . at
I'm in London and that's a fact
My horse and me have lots to see
This great town is the place for me

Yeehah, I'm rocking' and a rollin' down the street
I'm lookin' kinda busy but I'm still on my feet
Trippin' and troopin' tired buckarooin'
That's what makes me . . . me

Who's . . . who? What's . . . what?
Now I think I know you a lot
You must believe me, we will get along
I'm a cowgirl and that's the meanin' of this song

Yeehah, I'm rocking' and a rollin' down the street
I'm lookin' kinda busy but I'm still on my feet
Trippin' and troopin' tired buckarooin'
That's what makes me . . . me.

Kerry Jones (10)
Cleves School

A Sting In The Tail

Oggy, oggy, oggy
Wasps, wasps, wasps
Oggy, oggy, oggy
Wasps, wasps, wasps
Oggy
Wasps
Oggy
Wasps
Oggy, oggy, oggy
Wasps, wasps, wasps!

They thundered onto the field
Like a gladiator with a shield
Willing to take a chance
Against the men of France
With the support of their fans
And the rhythmic bands

The roaring of cheers
And the smell of beers
The ball in the air
High over there
Over the posts
Now we can boast!

Two minutes left on the clock
And the wasps were in shock
Toulouse had evened the score
And then we heard a roar
A last minute try
And we jumped high in the sky!

Oggy, oggy, oggy
Wasps, wasps, wasps!

Maddie Graeme (11)
Cleves School

The Lion

The lion paces up and down the cold, wet cage
His eyes shining bright,
Why am I here? he asks himself,
As the day turns to night.

He sleeps soundlessly in the cold wet cage,
As the moon rises high,
His long mane rustling in the breeze,
As the night-time passes by.

When he wakes in the cold wet cage,
He tries to forget why he's here,
How the poachers came and tracked him down
And struck him full of fear.

They tied him up with chains and ropes
And whipped him when they could,
They brought him to his cold wet cage
And left him there for good.

So now he lies in the cold wet cage,
Starving and longing to be free,
He always wonders what he did wrong,
Well, nothing if you ask me . . .

Greg McAllister (11)
Cleves School

Wind

Strong as a bull the wind sails,
Round every corner,
Always everywhere at once,
Unexplainable,
Leaves drop off the trees in autumn,
Because of the wind,
Ships sail then sink 'cause of wind.

Lydia Whittle (10)
Cleves School

My Grandad

Gets his paper with his ticket,
Watches football, rugby and cricket.
He's thoughtful and helpful, does the best he can,
A loving and caring kind of man,
He's into cars in every way,
He's a challenge to Schumacher any day.

He's been to Arabia, Spain and France,
He even gave Australia a chance!
He's a wow with a paintbrush, saw and drill,
He adores our pets Harry and Will,
Anything you ask him he will know,
But on the River Dee he gets me to row!

He loves my grandma from head to toe,
If you could see him now it would show,
But he loves all in the same way,
I wouldn't change him any day!

Hannah Mitchell (11)
Cleves School

Summer To Autumn

As all wet weather fades away,
The summer sunshine comes to stay.
The days are long, the evenings light,
A great time for a water fight!

Summer PJs, skirts and shorts,
Flowers grow - all different sorts.
Barbeques will soon be gone,
Say bye to the sun, the way it shone!

It's autumn now, when flowers die
And crispy leaves fall from the sky.
As leaves keep falling from up high,
This poem is ending till winter - goodbye!

Julia Niemann (11)
Cleves School

My Pet

My pet rock
Lives in a sock,
He sleeps all day
And never runs away.

My pet rock
Is called Jock,
He's not very fluffy
But is a big toughie.

My pet rock
Can't undo a lock,
I thought he would starve
When I found him in the Algarve.

My pet rock
Is part of my stock,
He's my favourite one,
We're always having fun.

My pet rock
Isn't part of a flock,
He's one of a kind
And he's my greatest find!

Jordan Horsford (11)
Cleves School

Chocolate Cake!

You love or hate chocolate cake!
If you eat too much you put on weight
You think it's yummy, but it hurts your tummy
When you're sick, it's not funny.

Dark chocolate cake is very rich
If you hate it you'll have to ditch
Milk chocolate cake is the best
Have a slice and have a rest.

Victoria Hamilton (10)
Cleves School

Why Does It Always End Like This?

There goes the whistle, the end of extra time
It's a shoot-out, what could be worse?
The European Cup and it's a shoot-out,
Their captain is the first penalty taker,
He steps up and puts it in the top corner.
Now it's our top scoring striker,
He steps up and it's in the goal,
Next penalty taker for them looks confident and puts it away,
Now our turn, we must score this,
He steps up and puts it away,
Now it's their last person who looks nervy and unstable,
He's in the box and he misses,
Now it's my turn, I'm nervous, my knees are shaking,
If this goes in we've won the cup,
I'm aiming for top right,
I fool the keeper and go the other way,
We've won, we've won the cup,
We step up to take the cup,
Champions of Europe.

Tom Frost (11)
Cleves School

My Beanstalk

My beanstalk is like Jack's but better,
I leave it on the window sill through the day
And at night I climb until I reach cloud 2,
Cloud 2 is full of children who like me, have beanstalks,
It's a magical candyland with big slides and swings,
If Jack had climbed just a little bit higher
He wouldn't have been chased by that horrible giant.

So remember if you get a beanstalk
Follow the signs to cloud 2.

Chloe Mackenzie (11)
Cleves School

The Battle

Dong Zhuo, king and warlord of the Luo Yang stands ready
to face the enemy,
From the walls of his city on the snowy plains of Zhongei Province,
Men hidden in the far-away mountain waiting to carry out ambush,
The enemy charge,
Mounted horsemen fall to the floor,
Ram down and through the first gate come the enemy,
Pikes and swords clash together,
Lu Bu, office of Dong Zhou
Strikes out on the second gate,
Killing a number of men straight away,
Lu Bu gets wounded and withdraws from battle,
His men manage to kill Diou Chan,
But the enemy battle on,
They break into the castle,
Dong Zhuo sets it on fire,
Deciding to escape out the back of the castle.

Oliver Barry (11)
Cleves School

Alone

As I stand at my post,
I see young and old fight for what matters most.
Sometimes limbs are broken,
Or new pride awoken,
But I just stand there as the skipper,
As a field now goes past their wall, they bring in their ripper,
The ripper attacks, our man is down,
We take a shot and my opposite number is made a clown,
The game is almost up, the opposition launch an attack,
A shot comes into my right, I dive and save it,
The crowd shouts 'Mack!'
I am a hero, my team has won, as I lift the trophy,
The crowd shout 'Goalie!'

Jordan Palmer (11)
Cleves School

Unique

You are unique until someone comes along,
This someone asks you if you will become famous and sing a song,
You agree quite happily,
Your friends come to the concert joyfully,
But to their surprise they find everyone wearing the same khaki
                              clothes and doing your exact same pose,
You now are disappointed,
This isn't what you wanted,
So you walk off stage and down your cheek runs a tear,
You know this is the end of your new career,
Next day you wake up and go down the street,
But no one at all that you meet
Is wearing the same khaki clothes
Or doing the exact same pose,
Then from behind you hear a voice
And when you turn around you see a person wearing the same
                              clothes and doing your same pose,
Then you realise that you're not cool,
To all these people you're just plain old you.

Zoe Woodbridge (11)
Cleves School

The Seaside

T ravelling across land, waiting for water,
H alfway there, 'Hurry up Dad, you're going too slow.'
E nchanting view from upon the cliff, 'Are we nearly there yet?'

S ea shimmering, water blue, oh what a lovely day,
E njoying the atmosphere, buzzing with fun,
A ll ages invited, children screaming, adults chatting,
S un shining in the cloudless sky, hot and breezy,
I ce creams all around, to help cool off, what a treat,
D riving back home, everyone tired, oh what a lovely day,
E njoying the atmosphere, sunset and all, what a lovely treat,
   oh what a lovely day.

Becky Cummins (11)
Cleves School

Sandy Words

I'm playing by the deep blue sea,
There's no one here except for me.
I'm making sculptures in the sand,
And watching ships come into land.

I strap my swimsuit on and run,
I'm glad I am the only one.
The breeze is blowing in my face,
I know this is my favourite place.

It's getting late; the sun's in bed,
The glowing moon is out instead.
The twinkling stars are with the moon,
It's going to be midnight very soon.

I swim out to sea in my rubber ring,
Until I see a weird thing.
It's triangular and its point so sharp . . .
Oh help, it's the fin of a *great white shark!*

I swim as fast as I can go,
Trying hard to touch the sand below.
That shark had given me such a fright,
Thank goodness it is out of sight!

Or is it?

Hannah McGregor-Viney (10)
Cleves School

Beyoncé Rules

Beyoncé you're the best,
Better than all the rest,
Forget J-Lo and Blue,
Because Beyoncé, I love you!
Your CDs are the bomb,
So is your website - Beyoncé.com!
Just go with your fab flow,
You'll always rock the show.

Amy Scott (11)
Cleves School

Looking Out Of My Bedroom Window

Looking out of my bedroom window,
I hear the beautiful humming of the birds and bees,
I see a party with music and laughter,
Looking out of my bedroom window,
I see my garden with bushes, flowers,
Plants and a wooden Wendy house.
I also see an old rusty swing,
I see children playing near the cars
And houses in the street,
In the clear blue sky
I see some tiny clouds with the sunlight blinding through,
A loud plane passes over my head
As I write this line,
I see wonderful wildlife here, there and everywhere,
I see lots of people at the party,
I see my old football on the soft, damp, grass,
That is what I see and hear
When I look out of my bedroom window.

Amy Williams (10)
Cleves School

The Ugly Old Man

He's tall and very fat,
He looks as grubby as a front doormat
Let's start with his hair
It was long, greasy, curly
Oh, all I could do was stare
Move down to his nose
It was dripping like a leaking hose
As for his skin
It was scaly like a fish's fin
He has a long drooping beard
I have to say it is all very weird
That is all I found
This time round.

William Prentice (11)
Cleves School

Black Shadow

Black shadow
Black shadow
Creeping through the night
Black shadow
Black shadow
Keeping out of sight

Over and under
In and out
What to do
He has no doubt

Backwards, forwards
Running through the night
He runs
Then stops, ready for a fight

He bares his teeth
Unsheathes his claws
The little mice stop and gaze in awe

Genocide, murder
Call it what you like
The deed he did
On that cold night.

Rhiannon Evans (11)
Cleves School

Rainbow

R ain and sun together make,
A beautiful sight like in a dream,
I n the sky a set of colours shining,
N othing can stop the wonders,
B efore you is a rainbow,
O h try to find the pot of gold,
W hen rain and sunshine meet.

Sarah Kernoghan (11)
Cleves School

Summer Poem

Summer's when new buds open
And when new flowers reproduce.

Summer's when the sun is out
And when the sky is blue.

When children play by the sun,
Whilst they're having fun.

Children get to stay at home
Without school for two whole weeks,

During then girls go for shopping sprees,
Whilst boys stay and chill.

Drinking juice and ice slush
And the strawberry milkshake (crush).

When summer ends, tears come from eyes
And all the rain and hail comes from the skies.

Now it's ended, autumn has come,
A whole new season has begun.

Asia Castle (10)
Cleves School

In The Park

Children singing
 Birds chirping
  Teenagers talking
   Adults walking
    Grass swaying
     Leaves rustling
      Plants growing
       Trees blossoming

Woodpeckers are pecking
 Larks are lurking
  All life is real
   When inside the park.

Lauren Berridge (11)
Cleves School

Mr Nobody

When Mum asks us (crossly),
'Whose fingerprints are those on the wall?
Whose books are those battered and torn?
Whose muddy footprints are those on the floor?'
We tell her,
'It was Mr Nobody.'

When Dad asks us (in a rage),
'Who's ripped a hole in my favourite shirt?
Whose idea was it to hide my slippers under the car?
Who's been giving the dog cereal for breakfast?'
We tell him,
'It was Mr Nobody.'

When our parents ask us (at boiling point),
'Who's burnt down the entire kitchen?
Who's promised our neighbours £100 each?
Who's bought a year's supply of sweets with our money?'
We tell them,
'It was Mr Nobody.'

For some reason our parents don't believe us
And they're grounding us for a year!
Even though we keep telling them Mr Nobody was here!
Oh well, at least you still believe us, don't you?

Salma Haddad (11)
Cleves School

My Grandad Is The Best

My grandad is the best
And he's even ninety-seven
But he thinks that I'm a pest
And he wants to be eleven

He runs and shouts, 'I'm young again!'
He ran the London marathon
My friends say he's cool in my secret den
But he's got a weird name, Garon

He always boasts about his skill
And Grandma always kisses him
I really think he's taking pills
He says, 'Are you okay, Tim?'

'Just be normal!' I scream at high pitch
When Grandad turned around
'Don't worry Son, we can be rich'
He dropped some money that he found

I said, 'Where'd you get that from?'
When he grabs me with his flabby arms
I shout to my dad, 'Where are you Tom?'
He chokes me to death, I hope for an alarm
I black out seeing a light which gleams
I wake up knowing it's a dream.

Sam Fisher (11)
Cleves School

Mirror

Mirror, mirror on the wall
Why do you not talk at all?
Why do you not laugh and joke
Is it that you are broke?
Mirror, mirror on the wall
Why do you not talk at all?

Mirror, mirror on the wall
Why do you not talk at all?
Could it be that you're sad
Or could it be you're mad?
Mirror, mirror on the wall
Why do you not talk at all?

Mirror, mirror on the wall
Why do you not talk at all?
If you talked what would you say?
Do you think that I'm okay?
Mirror, mirror on the wall
Why do you not talk at all?

William Marsh (11)
Cleves School

The Moon

The moon is a giant ball of rock
Which lies very high in the sky
One day it will be a full round ball
The other days it will be only one half
When the sun goes down, the moon comes up
And twinkles in with all the stars
But when dawn breaks and the sun rises up
The moon goes down again
We do not see it for a very long time
Until it's dark again
Until it's dark again.

Fouad Halawi (11)
Cleves School

Ambitions

I want to . . .

Catch a falling star and put it in my pocket
Take my eyeball out of my socket
Live forever, never die
Jump off a building and start to fly
Jump into fire and come out just fine
Win the lottery for the hundredth time
Jump through a brick wall and come out the other side
Become invisible to the naked eye
Gain the world's trust in just a day
Say all the things that I should say
Fly a plane without any experience
Never feel bad or delirious
Become a billionaire in the blink of an eye
Become famous without having to try
Have crazy ambitions, real hopes and dreams
Not just everyday things like these!

Diba Rahmani (11)
Cleves School

Anger

Anger is a thumping feeling inside
Anger eats away at you forever
Your face turns an evil red
Anger is something you would hate
Anger is a blood-drinking pain
Anger bubbles at your brain
Anger is everlasting trouble
Anger is a trouble sleeper
Anger is a head wall-banger.
Anger is a brain teaser!

Jade Nash (11)
Cleves School

The Circus!

The carnival has come to town,
With lions, tigers and some clowns.
The noise that is made shakes the ground,
When the elephants come marching round!

People walking all around,
Taking in the sights and sounds.
Jugglers juggle knives without a care,
Acrobats go flying through the air!

The ringmaster stands and looks so proud,
He cracks his whip so loud.
The crowd hush as the lights go dim
And wait for the magical show to begin!

The crowd all look up at the trapeze,
Watching the acrobats fly with ease.
Jaws drop at the tightrope walker,
The lion tamer looks like he's up for the slaughter!

The bareback horse-riders please and thrill,
The daring stunts almost cause a spill.
The clowns come out and the crowd are glad,
There was laughing and singing, they were really quite mad!

Now the show is over, everyone goes home,
The big cats are put in cages with nowhere to roam.
These animals that were once so proud,
Should this really be allowed?

Sophie Martin (11)
Cleves School

The Winding Road To Portugal

As the players pack their bags
The tension is growing around the country
With the players go the supporters
And all cram into Portugal.

On match day all the crowd
Come to cheer with their programmes in their hands
As they wonder who will play
Beckham? Butt? Bridge?

Game by game the competition hots up
As the teams try to reach the final
But who will win
France? England?

The supporters sing the songs
And fill in their wall charts
They wear their colours with pride
And faithfully fly their flags.

Back at home the whole country is watching
With highs and lows
Frustration and delight.

Hoping that they can win Euro 2004.

Lawrence Burden (10)
Cleves School

Getting The Bird

Bouncing, hopping
Happily along,
Twittering sweetly
Singing its song.

Blackbird chirping
In its nest,
Lungs nearly bursting
In his chest.

Cat slyly slipping
Up the tree,
Always wishing
To fill her tummy.

Crouching safely
On a branch,
Eyes focussed
On a scrumptious lunch.

Bird tweeting,
Cat spying,
Cat leaping,
Bird flying.

Blackbird soaring
Through the air,
Outwitted the cat
Then and there!

Cat staring
At her flying feast
He escaped from me
The little beast!

'I'll get you next time!'
The poor kitten miaowed,
'Oh well,' she sighed,
'I'll go eat my cat food!'

Kaylin Purvor (11)
Cleves School

Chimney Cheep

(Based on a true story)

Cheep cheep, what's that?
It was coming from the house
Whatever could it be?
It sounded like a mouse

Flutter flutter, no, that's not right
I know it sounds absurd
But I had a funny feeling
That it could be a bird

I searched for hours, and hours, and hours
And finally found the nest
It was up our unused chimney breast
And you can guess the rest!

Suddenly, in a puff of soot
A fledgling tumbled down
A darling baby blue tit
All blue and black and brown

No sooner had I stopped to think
When another one arrived
And then another, and another
Together there were five

The frantic mother flew about
As each new chick emerged
She called to them, on and on
'Try and fly' she urged

And one by one the tiny birds
Took off into the sky
Following their parents
'Goodbye' I heard them cry.

Phoebe Parnian (11)
Cleves School

The Jail Cell

I smell the mouldy porridge
They expect us to eat.

I hear the people scream and plead
When they have been locked up.

I feel I am going crazy
In this tiny room.

I taste the last good meal I had
A very long time ago.

I see the same old bars of metal
With the lock that keeps me in.

I want to come out.

I want to be free.

I am innocent! but no one believes me.

Charlotte Scott (11)
Cleves School

Weather Or Not

The weather's fine, the weather's great
Because it's sunny all through the day.
Everybody's going to the beach,
Having fun in the sun,
Putting lotion on , not to get burnt,
While others are in the park.

The weather's fine, the weather's worse
Because it's raining and so cold.
Staying at home watching TV,
Trying to pass time for the rain to stop.
The sun's come out but the rain's still there
And now you can see the rainbow shine.

Mike Elsayed (10)
Cleves School

A Perfect Witch's Potion

Tip some human's blood in the pot
Say the magic words a lot

Then dip in a toad's tongue
And make sure the toad is very young

Leave it for a certain time
And you should say a little rhyme

Sieve in some tadpoles' eyes
And add some flies

The recipe should be as green
As a piece of lettuce

Take some bloodthirsty vampire teeth
But try not to be a thief

If you are a human, never drink it
If you want to try some, just have a bit!

Holly Jones (10)
Cleves School

The Ancient Tree

I've been entrenched in the soil for many years
I am tall but my trunk is wizened and my branches gnarled
In spring my leaves unfurl, bright and bold, like a new beginning
On hot summer days my leaves make a green umbrella
Giving coolness and relief from the sun
In autumn, my leaves lose life and spiral to the ground
In winter I'm quiet and still like a lifeless object
Foxes rummage through the grass beneath my branches
Children clamber carelessly along my body
Many people have sheltered from the rain beneath my boughs
Most of my friends have fallen and withered
But I carry on alone, solid and wise.

Jonathan Tye (11)
Cleves School

Rapunzel - The True Story

As soon as Rapunzel began to think,
She said to herself, 'This place stinks!
I want to get out and meet the males
And give that witch a turn of the tale.'
So as soon as a prince came along,
It hit Rapunzel with a gong,
'This man will get me out.'
So she let out a snorty shout,
'Princey, Princey, get me down,
I want to get back on my throne, with my crown.'
The prince shouted back, 'OK, wait right there,
I'll be back with a ladder to show I care.'
No sooner had he left the scene,
The witch came along feeing quite keen.
'This silly prince is going to be mine,
He can cook, so he'll be fine.'
She got on her broom, thinking, *I'll be miz*
And then she was there in a spark and a whizz.
With Rapunzel snared, she was hid across town,
To a different tower where she couldn't be found.
The witch then waited for another hour,
Until the prince came back to the tower.
He climbed up the ladder, where he met his fate,
He brought down the witch and they arranged a date.
So the witch got her man, the prince got his girl,
But what about Rapunzel? Now that's a whirl!
In the tower she waits for her guy,
To rescue her before she dies.
This version of Rapunzel's story is true,
Not some fairy tale, specially done for you.

Ellie Johnson (11)
Cleves School

Emotions

Love is a room full of flowers,
It feels like a fur coat wrapped around you when you are cold,
Its colour is pink,
It tastes like strawberry ice cream,
Love looks like a butterfly.

Hatred is a volcano burning inside you,
It feels like a sharp stab creating pain inside,
Its colour is black,
It tastes like fire,
Hatred looks dark and mean.

Embarrassment is a scared emotion,
It feels like your best friend telling everyone your secrets,
Its colour is blushing red,
It tastes like fear,
Embarrassment looks like a red tomato.

Anger is a volcano erupting,
It feels like hot tar,
Its colour is scarlet purple,
It tastes like stones crunched up,
Anger looks like blood.

Sadness is a tornado,
It feels like you have shrunk,
Its colour is a lonely blue,
It tastes mean and unfair,
Sadness looks like a lonely tree.

Zoë Webb (10)
Cleves School

Aren't Brothers Lovely . . . !

(Dedicated to my brother, Jack)

Aren't brothers lovely . . .
How their feet smell of 2-year-old cheese
Their rooms smell like rotting compost
And their school shirts smell of BO

Aren't brothers lovely . . .
When the older ones tell you spooky stories
That you know aren't true
But because they are so scary
You can only manage to get to sleep when it's time for school

Aren't brothers lovely . . .
When they are smaller and younger
They let you have the blame for *everything*
Cry to look innocent
When it's something they have done

Aren't brothers lovely . . .
It's as if God made them just to annoy
Just to pong, push and pick their noses
They are like monkeys in a zoo

Aren't brothers lovely . . .
When they are older and protect you
And teach you things that are new
When they're younger, they are cute and cuddly
And they are there to have fun when you are bored
The best thing about them is that they put up with sisters like me
That's what brothers are for!

Helen Revell (11)
Cleves School

Seasons

S pring flowers, being planted,
P lants begin to pop up out of the soil,
R emembrance Day, celebrated by people wearing poppies,
I ce is melted and turned into water,
N aughty children picking the flowers,
G rowing flowers, all over again.

S plashing in paddling pools begins,
U ntil April showers come,
M ums eating their food outside,
M other birds hatching eggs,
E aster bunny is hiding eggs,
R unning athletes, getting worn out.

A utumn clothes being worn,
U nder the trees the leaves scatter,
T wirling leaves falling through the air,
U nderground creatures are hibernating,
M others are raking the leaves away,
N ights getting darker and darker.

W eather is cold and icy,
I ced over ponds where ducks are flying away,
N oel is sung by the Christmas choirs,
T insel hangs from Christmas trees,
E xcitement because it's Christmas time,
R unning children throwing snowballs.

Hannah Wilder (11)
Cleves School

Dragons

Many people say that dragons are unknown
Never to be discovered and never to be flown

Even though they are ancient
Still no one believes that dragons are still living
Flying high and running free

Many people say that dragons are unknown
Never to be discovered and never to be flown

Many people still don't know that dragons have no weakness
That neither man or beast will ever see
Without going into their caves while they're running wild and free

Many people say that dragons are unknown
Never to be discovered and never to be flown

Many people still don't know that they have fiery breath
That even kills the best of kings
And burns them to their deaths

Many people say that dragons are unknown
Never to be discovered and never to be flown

But dragons are still living
Although you might not see them
They prefer your dreams to real life
And that is where you'll see them!

Jessica Day (11)
Cleves School

Penalty Shoot-Out

I wish I could score,
I wonder what will happen,
Will I hit the back of the net?
I'm really not too sure.

Everyone is cheering,
I wonder what will happen,
I place the ball on the spot,
Will I score
Or will I not?

I'm ready to shoot,
I wonder what will happen,
I aim my shot
And swing my leg,
Oh my god, I wish I was dead!

I've kicked the ball,
I wonder what will happen,
The goalie dives to the right,
Yessssss!
Celebrations tonight!

My teammates are
Following me up,
I lift the cup,
I lift the cup,
Yessss!
Yessss!
Yessss!

Joshua Hamman (10)
Cleves School

Ikea

Today we went to Ikea,
To buy shelves was the idea,
But other things seem to come alive,
Like spicy herbs and mild chives.
They wandered into our trolley,
With other things such as lollies.
My mother bought two new bins
And crayons and pens just for Fin.
In and in the items came,
Even toys the exact same!
Pillows, fabrics, Swedish biscuits,
Finding our trolley, well you couldn't miss it!
We added clocks and lots of glass
And found we even needed fake grass!
I put in some lovely frames,
But my brother said they were really lame.
We sat and rested for a while,
Because it felt we had walked a mile.
The time had come for us to leave,
Just when Ikea started to heave.
We got to the till and paid our bill,
It wasn't too much,
Just a little over a hundred or such,
The funny thing was that . . .
We only went in for some shelves!

Beatrice Robjohn (11)
Cleves School

Neglected?

I lie in a handbag,
Quiet as a mouse.
When somebody dives
Deep inside my home.
I think I'm going to be free
As I gather all excitement,
But suddenly I'm picked up,
Moved then dumped.
Dumped inside the handbag,
A chance for forty winks.

Suddenly I wake,
Singing my favourite tune,
Louder and louder.
I think I'm going to be answered,
But nobody answers.
I guess I just can't be found deep,
Inside this cluttered hole.
Then finally I'm answered,
Happy again,
But then dumped, dumped back,
Inside my home, the deep dark hole,
The handbag.

Elloise Pepperrell (11)
Cleves School

The Dragon

He's banging on the floor
He's flying around the room
The dragon that lives next door
I hope he stops soon

Sometimes he likes to eat
His favourite meal is fish
He likes to eat with his feet
So he doesn't have to use a dish

The dragon has huge green eyes and sharp teeth
His skin is spiky and knobbly
No one knows what else lies beneath
The dragon's big fat body

He's getting quieter now
I can't stand him anymore
I really don't know how
That dragon can live next door.

Stephen Chinnadorai (11)
Cleves School

The Deepest Sea

The sea laps up against the beach
Eroding the rocks and sand away
It can be fierce with big strong waves
Gentle when it's calm and ripples.

Deep below the sea
Sea life swims and crawls about
Feeding and birthing
There's plenty to see.

Deep, deep down in the deepest
Black sea lies Neptune guarding
His shipwreck and treasure
No one knows he's there.

Ben McClaskey (10)
Cleves School

Footy

Football flying kicked by Henry,
Upward rushing hit the goalpost,
Now it's a corner, Gerrard takes it,
Heads it in by Michael Owen.

Jerzy Dudek takes the goal kick,
Zola heads it, Beckham kicks it,
Roy Keane passes it to Scholes,
Scholes scores a terrific goal!

Now it's two-nil, ha, ha, ha,
Foul, foul, penalty,
Hyppia takes the penalty,
Kewell scores with an overhead kick.

Sheringham takes the centre pass,
Passes it to Alan Shearer,
Five minutes till the end of the match
And Christiano Ronaldo celebrates with a fantastic goal!

It's the end of the match
Ha, ha, ha!
The score is four-nil!
Ha, ha, rah!

Kerry Liu (10)
Cleves School

Paradise

P is for palm trees swaying in the summer breeze,
A is for ambling along by the sea,
R is for the rock pools scattered around,
A is for alone, without a sound,
D is for dolphins as they twist and turn,
I is for images of paradise for which I yearn,
S is for sunbathing in the warm summer sun,
E is for Eden through which I run.

Katherine Maxwell (11)
Cleves School

There Is Heaven In Her Eyes

There is a heaven in her eyes,
Where goddesses and gods rest;
A fearless sorrow dies,
Wherein all pleasant souls rest;
There may be cries
But that's where all sorrow dies.

There soft clouds do enclose
That soft goodness is in her eyes,
Which when up close it really shows,
But when afar would paralyse.

Her eyes so heavenly watch them still,
Her brows like bended bows do stand still,
Her frightful tears really would kill,
For no mere mortal can resist her face,
For it can never be replaced.

Luke Boyd (11)
Cleves School

Sea

The waves crashing against the high mountains
Like a hungry cheetah eating bit by bit
The small boats in the distance getting thrown here and there
The house abandoned at the shore wearing down to a pile of rubble

When he is in a good mood the water will turn calm and clear
When he is in a bad mood no one wants to be near his
                                         rough dirty water

The sand fine and yellow, running into the sea
The sea collecting it and turning it a mud brown.

Robyn Davies (10)
Cleves School

I Hate Spiders

Jumping spiders,
Bloodthirsty,
Their first meal is their own mother,
Eight-legged freaks.

A scary, hairy experience,
Don't mess with them.
They'll only get mad!
Deadly poisonous spiders,
I hate spiders.

Tarantulas creep everywhere,
They can wall-crawl weaving webs,
Everywhere they pass they can see the world
All at once,
They are like acrobats.

Toby Lawson (9)
Educare Small School

Scary Spiders

Terrifying tarantula,
Creepy wet stingers,
Always alone the black widow thin and twig-like legs,
Still, like a frozen piece of ice,
Deadly poisonous spiders.

Enough eyes to see the world at once,
Dew hanging off the wet grass that looks like glittery pearls
And when the sun shines, it looks like a bar of gold
And eight legs to run super fast on.

Lily Yorke (10)
Educare Small School

Skipping

Skipping, skipping
Jumping, jumping
Over the jump rope line
When you skip
Doing your tricks
Jumping up and down
Jumping to and fro
Skipping is my hobby you know
Skipping!

Hannah Oxford (7)
Educare Small School

The Deadly Spiders

Terrifying tarantulas in dark creepy corners,
Eight-legged freaks,
Creepy web swingers,
Always alone, the black widow,
A scary hairy experience.

Decorate the flowers,
Acrobatic daredevils,
A web that sparkles and glints in the sunlight,
Enough eyes to see the world.

Dion Allen (8)
Educare Small School

Wall-Crawling Spider

The wall-crawling acrobatic daredevil,
Decorates the flowers with winding webs
Dew on the web like glittery pearls

There are creepy ones
With twig-like legs
The spooky black widow
Eats her own mate
That must be a scary hairy experience
Think about the terrible scary hairy tarantula!

Harrison Parker (8)
Educare Small School

Book

Book, a portal to another world
In disguise
Travel through time
See the world
Play with princesses and princes
Become a secret agent
Explore castles
Meet dragons and witches
Then close the book
Back to reality.

Liberty Blackmore (11)
Educare Small School

The Plains Of Africa

So swiftly does the lion run
Shaking his shaggy mane
Most beasts call him Mr Fame
The fiercest of all beasts
He'll cut your throat
It's best if you leap over the moat
Start the boat!
Oh no! He got you!

Pablo Linares-Bowles (11)
Educare Small School

Dogs

Dogs do
Jumping and running
Eating and everything
Some roll
Some rock
Bounce bounce
Woof woof
Bark bark.

Ollie Summers (8)
Educare Small School

Elves And Thieves

There once was a wolf with some loaves of bread,
Who went to the forest with five scarves on his head,
He bumped into elves on his way home,
The elves were thieves but left him alone,
He passed some calves and ran through leaves
And drank some halves in a pub called Elves and Thieves!

Lara Hyson (9)
Latchmere Junior School

Amulet
(Based on 'Amulet' by Ted Hughes)

Inside the polar bear's eye, the misty moon.
Inside the misty moon, the polar bear's paw.
Inside the polar bear's paw, the pure ice.
Inside the pure ice, the polar bear's fur.
Inside the polar bear's fur, the white snow.
Inside the white snow, the polar bear's ear.
Inside the polar bear's ear, the crunchy frost.
Inside the crunchy frost, the polar bear's blood.
Inside the polar bear's blood, the frozen river.
Inside the frozen river, the polar bear's mouth.
Inside the polar bear's mouth, the seal's tears.
Inside the seal's tears, the polar bear's eye . . .

Sarah Stacey (9)
Latchmere Junior School

Borrowing The Amulet
(Based on 'Amulet' by Ted Hughes)

Inside the lion's fang, the cold breeze.
Inside the cold breeze, the valley of fear.
Inside the valley of fear, the trickling stream.
Inside the trickling stream, the lion's heart.
Inside the lion's heart, the lion's throat.
Inside the lion's throat, the deer's tears.
Inside the deer's tears, the deer's blood.
Inside the deer's blood, the deer's heart.
Inside the deer's heart, the dark forest.
Inside the dark forest, the lion's fang.

Holly Milner (9)
Latchmere Junior School

In The Time Of The Hedgehog

(Based on 'In the Time of the Wolf' by Gillian Clarke)

Who sings the legend?
The hedgehog rustling the leaves,
The owl swooping in the trees,
The badger going to its burrow,
The mice in their cages.

Where can we read it?
In the high treetops,
In the heart of the mountains,
In the rays of the sun,
In a gust of wind.

How shall we keep it?
In the hollow tree trunks,
In the eyes of a wolf,
In the mind of a fox,
In the heart of nature.

How will we tell it?
With a strike of lightning,
With a bang of thunder,
With a shimmer of snow,
With a gasp of wind.

Gemma Annetts (8)
Latchmere Junior School

Borrowing The Amulet

(Based on 'Amulet' by Ted Hughes)

Inside the lion's fang, the misty sky.
Inside the misty sky, the golden river.
Inside the golden river, the lion's thick coat.
Inside the lion's thick coat, the furry mountain.
Inside the furry mountain, the lion's throat.
Inside the lion's throat, the deer's heart.
Inside the deer's heart, the voice of a dinosaur.
Inside the voice of a dinosaur, animals lay there crying!

Taylor Edgington (9)
Latchmere Junior School

In The Time Of The Wild Eagle

(Based on 'In the Time of the Wolf' by Gillian Clarke)

Who sings the legend?
The wild eagle in the moonlight,
The wild eagle in the wind,
The wild eagle in the heavens,
The wild eagle in the sun.

Where can we read it?
In the footprints of the legendary eagle,
In the shadow of the wild eagle,
In the heart of the gliding eagle,
In the forest of the swooping eagle.

How shall we keep it?
In the core of the volcano,
In the centre of the Earth,
In the unknown temple in the middle of the forest,
At the bottom of the sea.

Patrick McCarthy (8)
Latchmere Junior School

The Negotiation

I'd trade my father for a bat,
A big fat pig or a hairy rat,
A pink baboon or a scary house,
A limbering cat or a disgusting mouse,
I'd even trade him for a gnat,
A creaking door or an old hat,
A purple coat or a non-humped camel,
A knocking on a door or nothing at all,
A pencil case or a stupid telephone,
An exciting book or a ridiculous bone,
But I'd never trade him for another.

Erna Starr (9)
Latchmere Junior School

In The Time Of The Badger

(Based on 'In the Time of the Wolf' by Gillian Clarke)

Who sings the legend?
The crows in the cornfield
The snake in the sand
The sheep in the field
The hedgehog in the leaves.

Where can we read it?
In a petal of a rose
In the raindrops from the sky
In the snow from the mountains
In the reflection of the moonlight

How shall we keep it?
In the strike of lightning
In the tumbling river
In the beach's sand
In the leaves of a newly-grown tree.

How will we tell it?
With a grain of sand
With Earth's soil
With the ice from North Pole
With a shimmering.

Emilia Jagiello (9)
Latchmere Junior School

An Ode To Bluechoc

Oh hail Bluechoc!
I cannot ignore you,
I simply adore you.

When you enter my food hole
My heart sinks,
It only thinks . . . about you!

You chocolate-covered animal!
Your sticky outside,
Your sugary inside,
Your glistening wrapper,
How can I leave you?

Your unique shape,
Like a frog,
It's you that makes the world go round!

Your caramel inside,
Covered in blueberry,
Your smelly scent,
Oh hail! Oh hail!

You are my everything!
I love you!
I love you!

Ashna Gupta (10)
Latchmere Junior School

In The Time Of The Stallion

(Based on 'In the Time of the Wolf' by Gillian Clarke)

Who sings the legend?
The mole in the ground,
The eagle in the moonlight,
The bats in the mist,
The wind in the trees.

Where can I read it?
In a cloud in the sky,
In the leaf on a branch,
In the mist of the moon,
In the light of the sun.

How shall we keep it?
In the river of life,
In the voice of the adult,
In the ear of the infant,
In the box of the brain.

How will we tell it?
With a flash of lightning,
With a roar of thunder,
With a plucking of grass,
With a howl of wind.

Isabella Lindsley (9)
Latchmere Junior School

In The Time Of The Alligator

(Based on 'In the Time of the Wolf' by Gillian Clarke)

Who sings the legend?
The fish in the water,
The eagle in the sky,
The wolf in the forest,
The leopards in the trees.

Where can we read it?
In the mist of the forest,
In the moonlight of the night,
In the water of the stream,
In the whistle of the wind.

How shall we keep it?
In the river of the past,
In the wind of the night,
In the head of a child,
In the darkness of the sky.

How will we tell it?
With a bolt of lightning,
With a roar of thunder,
With a twist of the wind,
With a splash of the lake.

Luke Geraghty (9)
Latchmere Junior School

In The Time Of The Bear

(Based on 'In the Time of the Wolf' by Gillian Clarke)

Who sings the legend?
The owl in the tree
The mouse in the hole
The walls of his cave
The footprint in the snow

Where can we read it?
In the lake that he drank from
In the shadow in the snow
In the statues of the trees
In the animals that he killed

How can we keep it?
In the echo of his cave
On the floor that he slept on
In the heart of his cave
On the walls of his cave

How will we tell it?
Like he himself
In a rustle of a bush
From generation to generation.

Charlie Flowers (9)
Latchmere Junior School

In The Time Of The Badger

(Based on 'In the Time of the Wolf' by Gillian Clarke)

Who sings the legend?
The butterfly in the tree,
The frog in the pond,
The rabbit in the hole,
The owl in the moonlight.

Where can we read it?
In the spirits of the meadow,
In the flap of the eagle,
In the cry of the birds.

How shall we keep it?
In the memories of winds,
In the ripple of rivers,
In the bush of history,
In the voice of cubs.

How will we tell it?
With a crash of thunder,
With a whisper of life,
With a whoosh of a shooting star,
With a buzz of bees.

Kirsten Guest (8)
Latchmere Junior School

In The Time Of The Platypus

(Based on 'In the Time of the Wolf' by Gillian Clarke)

Who sings the legend?
The monkey in the forest,
The bats in the cave,
The tornadoes up the mountain,
The eagle in the moonlight.

Where can we read it?
In the mist of the sunrise,
In the strikes of lightning,
In the middle of a haunted house,
In the leg of a dinosaur.

How shall we keep it?
In the eye of a memory,
In the deepest of a cave,
In the plant of history,
In the stone of a brick.

How will we tell it?
With a smell of the wind,
With a crack in the enchanted stone,
With a roar of a lion,
With the tip of death.

Ross Morey (9)
Latchmere Junior School

In The Time Of The Tiger

(Based on 'In the Time of the Wolf' by Gillian Clarke)

Who sings the legend?
The owl in the current of the wind,
The fish in the heart of the sea,
The birds of the clouds,
The kings of the land.

Where can we read it?
In the icicles of winter,
In the flowers of summer,
In the rain of spring,
In the leaves of autumn.

How shall we keep it?
In the lakes of India,
In the mountains of Greece,
In the deserts of Egypt,
In the snow of the North Pole.

How will we tell it?
With a bang of thunder,
With a storm of Hell,
With a falling tree,
With a shot of a gun.

Daniel Meegan (8)
Latchmere Junior School

In The Midnight Hour

In the midnight hour, the special hour,
Secrets await.
High up in the sky, a feathery creature soars,
Owl aloft.
Deep down in his set, badger is digging,
Eyes alert.
Slinking along with a smooth fur coat, cat moves,
Legs astride.
A liquid gushes, in the light of the moon,
Water a-glitter.
A scented cup opens, that feels like silk,
Flower abloom.
A dreaming shape hidden under layers of material,
Human asleep.

In the midnight hour.

Leonie Maier (10)
Latchmere Junior School

What's Happening To Me?

I can hear the sound of a bird singing a soft tune,
The trees rustle and the blossom falls on me.
I look down at the damp earth and what should I see
But my gran's grave,
Covered in pink blossom,
I look up again and there was Dad gazing at me.

Then suddenly!
The darkness surrounds me,
The leaves rustle in the wind,
I can hear the sound of an owl hooting in the distance,
The howl of a wolf, like a child's cry.

What's happening to me?

Holly Clemens (10)
Latchmere Junior School

Water

Water is sometimes a she, a gentle one.
Her soft touch on your hair, her smooth skin against your cheek,
Her warmth fills the air, her visible hair is seen in her warmth,
She trickles down any object which blocks her destination,
She finally stops at the bottom where she has no communication.

Sometimes the water is a he, a sly one.
He splashes his hands and makes a loud roar,
He is a cheater, he takes the shortcut
And flattens any building or house which dares to stand in his way,
He spits out wrecks of the destroyed buildings on the bay.

Water is sometimes neither a he nor a she,
Its gentleness and slyness is mixed as it runs through the sea,
It twists and turns but is captured by the gentleness,
Water rushes and he pushes forward but she is left behind,
He has left her on her own, her own way to find.

Farah Malik (10)
Latchmere Junior School

Mishka

Mishka is a sneaky cat
And the cheekiest I know,
But she's funny and furry
And that's why I love her so.

She'll climb up the chimney
Or to my window sill,
But if Mishka gets frightened,
Her back arches like a hill.

Her fur is midnight black,
Her ears are smartly pricked,
Though if she thinks you need a clean,
You'll get briskly licked.

Rosanna Quigley (11)
Latchmere Junior School

If You Were Me, Where Would You Be?

If I were me two hundreds years back
This is perhaps where I'd be . . .

Sitting on crumbling steps lost and lonely,
Watching the world go by,
Horses and carts clatter past,
Splashing up murky puddles with loud hard shoes,
While inside the lavish assembly rooms,
I hear the sound of many elegant feet on a dance floor,
Cab drivers cough and sneeze in the cold night air,
Ladies in beautiful puffed ball gowns suddenly appear from
                                the assembly rooms
And step gently up into an awaiting cab,
While others pause to drop a penny or two
Into my begging, clasping hands,
Then the cab rumbles off into the darkness,
The London streets are quiet and lonely.

But if I me was I two hundred years from now
This is perhaps where I'd be . . .

Sitting in a car, comfortable and cosy,
Watching the London Eye,
Cars and vans zoom past,
Splashing up murky puddles with black sleek tyres,
While inside the throbbing disco
I hear the sound of many drumming feet on a dance floor,
Taxi drivers cough and sneeze in the cold night air,
Girls in stripy mini skirts suddenly appear from the disco
And step up into a convenient taxi,
The taxi rumbles off into the darkness,
The London streets are quiet and lonely.

If you were me
Where would you be?

Rachel Shannon (11)
Latchmere Junior School

Goldilocks And Her Partner In Crime

Goldilocks committed a crime,
Committed it for a second time.
But while she crept into the wood,
She came across Miss Riding Hood.

'Can I play a trick with you?
How about the woman who lives in a shoe?'
'Na, Red, you're far too good,
I'm going back to the bears, I should.'

So Goldilocks and her partner in crime
Went to raid the bears for a second time.
They went to the house by crossing a bridge
And when they broke in they attacked the fridge!

After thirty cans of Coke,
Goldilocks finally spoke,
'I feel bloated, let's sit down,
I'm getting the seat with a pointed crown!'

Up jumped the girls, they ran to the chair,
That belonged to Baby Bear.
They jumped on the chair and *crash*,
It fell to the ground all crumpled like ash.

'I'm tired now, let's go to bed,'
Goldilocks wearily said.
They jumped on a bed and with a loud sound,
Baby Bear's bed fell to the ground.

When the bears had come back, the girls had gone,
But the bears could smell Goldilocks' pong.
They chorused, 'Oh Goldilocks, by far
We know who your parents are!'

Michaela Betts (10)
Latchmere Junior School

Did You See The Witch's Cat?

Did you see the witch's cat?
The dark and spooky witch's cat
With its red eyes and its white teeth
That's the witch's cat.

Spooky I know and scary too
But that's the witch's cat
Don't go near the evil thing
He will scratch and bite your children
But that's the witch's cat

He's black all over, so you won't see him
He's very smooth, slick and slim
As he flits through the trees and leaves
He doesn't make a sound so you won't know he's around
But when you do, he gives you such a fright
With his terrifying miaow!

Gemma Downs (10)
Latchmere Junior School

Extinction

Where is the wind that whispers through the ages?
Where is the sea that beats upon the shore?
Where is the moon shining brightly?
Where is the wolf that calls so lowly?
Where is the robin singing slowly to the morning sky?
Where is the plant waving in the breeze?
Where is the snow falling so peacefully?
Where is the rain that beats so heavily?
Where is the sun that shines so brightly upon the Earth?

The world is so empty and lonely,
It's so empty like a bucket with a hole.

Gregory Winter (10)
Latchmere Junior School

Dreaming The Loch Ness Monster

Last night I dreamt the Loch Ness monster,
    darting through the lake.
Its whip-like tail curving round,
    splashing up jewels of water.

Last night I dreamt the Loch Ness monster,
    diving down deep under.
To the relaxed safety of its home,
    where it can have a dreamy rest.

Last night I dreamt the Loch Ness monster,
    sipping the shimmering water.
Its dazzling scales shining,
    in the scorching afternoon sun.

Last night I dreamt the Loch Ness monster,
    with a box on my bedside table
And deep inside it was
    a shiny rainforest-green scale.

Thomas Hearn (9)
Latchmere Junior School

An Ode To My Pencil Case

Oh wonderful pencil case
What a pretty picture you have on your front,
What glamorous roomy space you have inside you.

Oh pencil case,
How fast your zip runs up and down your slim body
That keeps all my stuff in,
I shall always worship you forever,
If I was to mislay you
I would cry waterfalls.

Gareth Dean (9)
Latchmere Junior School

Animals

Hairy legs,
Teeth like pegs,
Sticky web,
Venomous bite,
Everyone should watch out for sneaky spiders;

Slithery body,
Covered in coils,
Muscles which squeeze,
Deadly poison,
Watch out for sinister snakes;

Paws and claws,
Super speeds,
Lovely coat,
Also a patient hunter,
Do not disturb wild cats;

Massive body,
Stomping feet,
A whip-like trunk
And giant spears called tusks,
Elephants can be very gentle though;

Size beyond all,
Strange teeth called baleen,
Its home is the ocean,
A graceful swimmer,
The calmest creature is the whale;

Poor senses,
They create war,
Short, pathetic nails,
Low speed,
Humans rely on guns.

William Conder (10)
Latchmere Junior School

What Is London All About?

The ding dong of Big Ben
The scream of the Tower of London
The pushing and shoving of Tower Bridge
The London Eye going round and round
This is what London is all about

Watching BBC on TV
Foxy on the radio
Reading Harry Potter
Playing on the computer
This is what London is all about

Fish and chips
Roast dinner too
Ice cream by the Thames
Hotdog on the tube
This is what London is all about

Sitting on the bench reading the papers
Waiting for the train
Hop on the bus
Get in the taxi into town
This is what London is all about

This is what London is all about
The man shouting, 'Evening Standard'
People rushing to and fro
This is what London is all about.

Nick Wood (10)
Latchmere Junior School

The Negotiation

I'd trade my brother for a sister,
A sweety shop or naughty blister,
A room of dirt, a bag of shells,
A soda pop, a block of bells,
I see you have a pile of books,
Just offer me one of those lovely hooks,
A wobbly tooth, an ice cream cone,
A flock of sheep, let me play that xylophone,
A tennis ball, a play toy snake,
A speckled frog, a Christmas cake,
I know that we can make a deal,
Oh look at that pencil, let me feel,
That child must go, tell him mister,
Please let me have a sister.

Katherine McLoughlin (8)
Latchmere Junior School

My Teachers Are Aliens

I will never understand them
They chat on mobile phones
And I think they speak in teacher-talk
Each one has their own.

They ambush each other in classrooms
And go off together at break
And eat lots of treats in cupboard
Especially KitKats and cake.

They like to go to the staffroom
And drink cups of coffee and tea
I think my teachers are aliens
And they're here in search of me!

Sarah Howden (9)
Latchmere Junior School

Trade Those For These

I'd trade my atlas for a bunch of daisies
A rubber lizard or a boy that's lazy
A box of Celebrations, a big bass drum
An electric guitar, a very nice mum
I see you have some Coke vanilla
I think you should swap it for my ninja killer
Just offer me a copy of Pokémon ruby

I'll trade my wig for a farmer's pig
A bag of shells, a bowl of twigs
A game or a broken leg
A ride on a train or a flight to Spain
I see you have some Milky Bar
I'll trade it for my racing car
For all these trades give me a copy of Pokémon ruby.

Samuel Kopinski (9)
Latchmere Junior School

Nature

Nature is a wonderful, lovely thing,
Listen to the birds and the way they sing.

The footsteps of the creatures,
The rustle of the leaves.

From giant roaring bears
To harmless little bees.

Nature gives us everything,
Summer, autumn, winter, spring.

It gives us rain, also shine,
It gives us weather, all the time.

Charlotte Seers (9)
Latchmere Junior School

Madame Tussauds

I looked at the stars,
One was from Mars,
I looked with surprise,
With my gleaming little eyes,
I said to my mum,
'Why look so glum?'
We went to the hall of horror,
Where James Bond was playing pool,
I was looking at a waxwork of Dover,
When I slipped and fell over.

Isabel Evans (8)
Latchmere Junior School

I Can Hear . . .

I can hear Dad settling to bed,
I can hear my mum breathing in her head,
I can hear a dog barking at the moon,
I can hear someone playing a tune,
I can hear Gareth parking his old car,
I can hear a geezer from afar,
I can hear the sounds at night,
Sometimes they give me a fright.

Lucy Mahoney (8)
Latchmere Junior School

Haiku

The dark cat pounces
The bright canaries scatter
Full cat licks his lips.

Robert Hayes (8)
Latchmere Junior School

Colours Around The World

In Scotland by black Loch Ness I feel excited,
On the beach on the corny yellow sand,
In the park playing on the lime-green grass and the
                              chocolate-brown tree trunks,
In London I can hear lots of cars and beeping buses in the blur,
In apple-green Ireland with all the leprechauns leaping around.
Hot orange Spain and its sun makes beads of sweat run
                              down your face.
Feeling the wind blow against my face in paper-white Iceland.
Watching the acrobats and people go past in plum-red China.
I'm really sad that I've got to go, but I'll come back one day I know.

George Faulkner (8)
Latchmere Junior School

HMS Victory

In England, Portsmouth, the HMS Victory lies,
Locked up in dirty water,
Which takes us back to the battle of Waterloo,
With the banging, blood, loud noises and the loss of lives,
But now we move on from that morbid thought,
So now it is in a dark dingy place,
When you go inside you can imagine the ship rocking
From side to side like you have been there already.

Nadir Adoul-Rutherfoord (9)
Latchmere Junior School

The Moon

The moon is a giant golf ball
That comes out when we are asleep
It shines so bright
And is so big
Like a giant night light
Up in the sky.

Louis Ekoku (8)
St Joseph's RC School, Epsom

The Moon

The moon is like a golf ball flying through the air,
It has loads of bumps and lumps,
But it doesn't really care,
It plays hide-and-seek with me and I count 1, 2, 3
And I say, 'Are you ready for little old me?'
Sometimes I find him when the sky is clear
And sometimes I don't,
I'll see you when the tiny twinkling stars are out and about.

Luke Haynes (8)
St Joseph's RC School, Epsom

The Moon

The moon is a piece of communion bread
That is pearl-white
In the mysterious mauve sky
Soundless and smiling
With its gentle face
The moon is a piece of communion bread.

Nicole Nartallo (8)
St Joseph's RC School, Epsom

The Moon

The moon is like a crystal ball
The way it shimmers and shines
Hanging high up in the sky
It brings light
To the dark and dismal night
Glittering and glowing
Above us all.

Giulietta Tallo (9)
St Joseph's RC School, Epsom

The Moon

The moon glows like a light bulb,
shining light across the night.

Guiding everybody on their way,
next to all the shiny stars.

Glowing in the darkness,
casting shadows through the night.

Always running from the sun.

Conor Bracken (9)
St Joseph's RC School, Epsom

The Moon That Sparkles

The moon looks like a golf ball
That shoots out
And rolls across the sky
Rolling and rolling
In the sky weaving around the stars
To me the moon looks like a golf ball
And then . . . it goes.

Niamh Donnelly (8)
St Joseph's RC School, Epsom

The Gleaming Golf Ball In The Sky

The moon is like a golf ball
That floats
Around our globe
It glints and gleams
And lights up our nights
With her shiny silver surface.

Daniel Diaz (9)
St Joseph's RC School, Epsom

The Moon

The moon is a shiny penny,
That someone flicks up into the dusk,
Where it stays until the next morning,
Then it falls back to Earth,
Back to someone's hands
And at night someone throws it back,
Up into the starry night,
Do you know what the holes in the moon are?
They are the place where someone's fingers have been!

Teresa O'Leary (9)
St Joseph's RC School, Epsom

The Moon

Shining like a football
Over a drifting sky
Round and round like a merry-go-round
Moving all the time
Spinning slowly in the starry sky
You give dreams to everybody
Could I kick you so high?

Dominic Roche (9)
St Joseph's RC School, Epsom

Marble

The moon is like a marble,
Big, round and bright,
It rolls very slowly,
All through the night,
When it shines down on me,
I say, 'What a sight
That marble is tonight!'

John Twells (9)
St Joseph's RC School, Epsom

My Brother Is A Monkey

I like monkeys like my friend
I like the way they twist and bend
I like the way they are very cheeky
The branches they swing on are extremely creaky

The dreadful thing is my brother is one
My mother and father must have had the wrong son
He sneaks bananas which he shouldn't do
He even eats flies with green goo

He is fabulously sneaky and very cheeky
He watches me and is very peeky
Please stop my brother being a monkey
Or when he is older he'll be very hunky.

Laura Cooke (9)
St Joseph's RC School, Epsom

Moonlight

One night I saw the moon
It looked like a disco ball
It shone down on me
Like a lighthouse light
Picking me out of the shadows
I felt as if I was captured by the moonlight.

James Hampshire (9)
St Joseph's RC School, Epsom

The Misty Moon

The moon's so high like a golf ball in the misty sky
And sometimes when I look at it, it looks like an apple pie
Bubbling and popping like popcorn in a pan,
The moon is the moon, amazing and white.

Conor Davison (8)
St Joseph's RC School, Epsom

The Moon

The moon is very round
People seem to think
That it makes a sound

The moon is like
A gigantic piece of cheese
And it is bigger than trees

But it is
Just my friend.

Daniel Schifano (9)
St Joseph's RC School, Epsom

The Moon

The moon's milky mask,
Smiles down on me,
Lighting up the night sky,
Beyond the twinkling stars,
Shimmering and glimmering,
Making her way across the sky,
With her bright reflections.

Andrew Doyle (9)
St Joseph's RC School, Epsom

The Moon

The moon is a white clock
That creeps about
From the large clouds
So that it can be seen
Silently and carefully
It disappears into the clouds.

Olivia Leitch (9)
St Joseph's RC School, Epsom

The Moon

The moon is a sparkling shell,
It follows me around when I am in the car,
It shines ever so bright with the stars at night,
It has holes in like a piece of cheese,
Sometimes it's round,
Sometimes it's thin,
I wonder what shape it will be tomorrow night?

Caitlin Rosbotham (8)
St Joseph's RC School, Epsom

Like The Moon

I am the moon, I'm up in the sky
Some people say that I can fly
Some people think that I'm a cheese
Or a UFO if you please!
Some people think that I'm a star
Or a flying Frisbee thrown too far
But all I am is rock and ice
And very, very, very nice!

Drew O'Hare (9)
St Joseph's RC School, Epsom

The Shining Pearl

The moon is a shining pearl
That comes out
From the sky
Only at night
All bright and cheerful
Looking at us
While we are sleeping tight.

Johnny Ciesco (8)
St Joseph's RC School, Epsom

The Magical Moon

The magical moon like a precious diamond,
Shines brightly in the sky,
It lights up our night like a massive night light,
It rises up when the sun goes down,
That's when we're all asleep
And then the sun rises up again,
To greet the morning light.

Fiona Hampshire (9)
St Joseph's RC School, Epsom

The Moon

The moon is a shining medal
Thrown right up in the sky
Its shining silver and glowing light
Is making the darkness all so bright
Like a firefly floating in the night
Moving around from left to right
As it disappears behind the clouds.

Elizabeth Dawe (9)
St Joseph's RC School, Epsom

The Moon

The moon's a spooky cat's eye
That furtively crawls
Between the clouds
Ducking and diving
Appearing and disappearing
Through the trees
Scary and mysterious is the moon.

Katie-Jane Hinksman (9)
St Joseph's RC School, Epsom

The Moon

The moving moon was shining brightly,
Like a silver ball in the sky,
A light at night,
Following you in the car,
Like a shadow,
High in the sky,
Looking down on you like a guardian.

Mario Raffa (9)
St Joseph's RC School, Epsom

Silver Shining Star

Up in the sky there's a silver star,
When I sleep I dream of it,
Glowing up the neighbourhood,
In the dark blue sky,
It makes me think of happy things,
Makes me think of a ten pence coin,
This silver shining star.

Grace McGovern (9)
St Joseph's RC School, Epsom

The Mystery Moon

The moon drifted through the starry pitch-black sky
Lighting up the world below
Like a shiny silver coin
Against the black velvet sky
Following me wherever I go.

Charlotte Cane (9)
St Joseph's RC School, Epsom

What Is It?

What is that big white ball in the sky?
It's like a light bulb up so high,
I hope it never goes away
Because I'd like to go up there
And touch it one day.
I would like to find out why
It comes out in the morning
And why it comes out again
When I'm yawning.

Charlie Gregory (9)
St Joseph's RC School, Epsom

Beth's Moon Poem

The moon is like a golf ball
High in the sky
The galaxy of stars the course
When the Earth and the sun come into line
The Earth is the hole and the sun is the trophy
One of the first men on the moon played golf that day
He said that his first step on the moon was small
But it was a giant leap for mankind.

Beth Smallwood (8)
St Joseph's RC School, Epsom

Homework

Homework is stupid, homework is bad,
All it ever does is drive me mad,
Last time we had three, now we've got four,
Every day we just get more and more.

My little sister always gets none,
Which means I miss out on all the fun.
It's totally stupid, it's not fair
That I should do homework, oh why should I care?

Ned, the class geek is the only one
That'll do homework than have heaps of fun,
Cos I don't have a reason that we should even try
To do this homework, oh why, oh why?

Then when we got our marks back from the test,
I got the worst, lower than all the rest,
But now I've learned my lesson that'll stay in my brain,
When I never did my homework and then felt the shame!

Sabina Wantoch (10)
St Mary's RC Junior School, Carshalton

Pentecost Poem

When the Holy Spirit came,
It brought a very huge flame.
One for each of the disciple's heads,
The flames were orange, yellow and red.
It came in a huge grey cloud,
Which made them speak languages aloud.
Italian, Russian, Chinese even Swiss,
Pentecost was a time you shouldn't miss,
They used this to spread Jesus' words,
To all different beings, even birds.
Now we should try and follow God's way,
All the time, in the past, future and today.

Meghan Looney (10)
St Mary's RC Junior School, Carshalton

Assessment

I have written an assessment
And no one knows what I meant
So I write and write
All through the night
I hand it in and my teacher stares
Then he takes the paper and he tears and tears
'What have you done? What do you mean?
Now I don't want you to be seen!'
'No Sir, no Sir, don't be mean.'
'But boy, you need to be more keen.'
So I stay in at play
And the teacher says, 'Are you really going to stay?'
'Yes Sir, yes Sir, I'm being keen!'
'Fine,' he said, 'I won't be mean,
You are dismissed
And don't think you will be missed!'

Katharine Woods (10)
St Mary's RC Junior School, Carshalton

My Friends

I have a friend called Jamie
I like him a lot
He has many things
And he wants what I have got

I have another friend called Adam
I think he is shy
He likes to eat chicken curry
And his dog eats flies

My other friend is James
And he is quite funny
He likes to play football
But he does not like bunnies.

Robert Powell (10)
St Mary's RC Junior School, Carshalton

Football Crazy

Football, football
It is great
Score a goal
To impress a mate

Football, football
It's so cool
Miss a shot
And be a fool

Football, football
It's so fun
Get to the wing
And make a run

Football, football
It's so mad
It can make you jumpy
It can make you glad.

Ryan Jenkins
St Mary's RC Junior School, Carshalton

Cheerleading Poem

C arshalton cheerleaders are
H yper and
E nergetic
E motional and we learn new
R outines
L oud and
E njoyable
A chievements just like
D ancing
I 'm
N utty about cheerleading and it's
G reat!

Leanna Goveia (10)
St Mary's RC Junior School, Carshalton

Help, I'm Scared

I'm all alone, my family's asleep,
What do I hear, a tapping sound?
Help, I'm scared
I'm going down to have a look
It's only the radiator

I'm all alone, my family's in bed
What do I hear, something dripping?
I go down the corridor
Help, I'm scared
It's only the tap

I'm in bed, my family's in bed
What do I hear, something wishing and swishing?
Help, I'm scared
It's coming from the next bedroom
Help, I might be under attack
I'm starting to feel a shiver running through my spine
Everything's gone quiet
Boo, help . . .
It was just my brother waiting for a chance to scare me

I'm snug up in my bedroom drifting off to sleep
Goodnight now, just wait one sec
There's just one thing I'm worried about
And that's what's behind my *bed*?

Joanna Ghobar (10)
St Mary's RC Junior School, Carshalton

Excuses

'Sir, I really need you,
I'm stuck on this first sum,
I've got a funny feeling
and it's near my tum,
I can't feel my legs, Sir
I think they're turning numb.

I've got a snotty nose, Sir,
My knees are shaking bad,
My friends are being horrible,
I'm feeling really sad,
I'm really, really tired, Sir,
I think I'm going mad!

The work is too hard, Sir,
I'm going to be sick,
I'm bored with the maths, Sir,
Get a bowl, quick!
Oh please Sir, don't let me suffer
I'm feeling really thick.

I feel really bad, Sir,
I feel all alone,
You need to phone my mum, Sir,
I'm just gonna moan.
I'm really, really drowsy, Sir,
So please may I go home?'

Jessica Mundy (10)
St Mary's RC Junior School, Carshalton

When I Was At Camp

When I was at camp,
In the middle of the night,
The field was damp
And I needed the loo.

I was sitting there, in the dark,
Thinking of what to do,
Then I heard a bark,
I jumped out of my skin.

Then I thought to myself, *you can do it!*
I then got out of my sleeping bag,
I was scared a bit,
Actually, scared a lot.

I stepped outside, facing my fears,
My torch making shadows,
Then I listened with my ears,
I thought I heard a wolf.

When I reached the toilets,
They were really horrible,
I wanted to go back and get
My little cuddly toy.

It was like it was never going to end,
When I got out of the toilets,
My insides started to bend,
I had to face the dark again.

Then I ran,
As fast as I could,
Then I accidentally kicked a can,
I was really scared.

Then I stood, staring,
I thought it was a monster,
Everyone was asleep, not caring,
It turned out to be a tent.

Then I hurried along,
To get to my tent,
I thought I heard a bong,
Then I knew I was imagining things.

When I got back to my tent,
I snuggled under my sleeping bag,
But then, oh no! I was so scared,
I needed the loo again!

Hannah Doyle (10)
St Mary's RC Junior School, Carshalton

Holy Spirit

In the attic sat the disciples
Scared and sad from Jesus' death,
Hiding from the Roman soldiers,
Too scared to take a breath.

'We're OK,' said Peter quietly,
'Though now I want to die,'
'I know how you're feeling,' said Luke
'And I really don't know why.'

Then in through the window came a wind
Then a blast of light
Fire settled upon their heads
As they sat there in fright.

'Fire,' Mark shouted out
'It's crackling, can you hear it?'
'No it's not,' shouted Simon
'It's the Holy Spirit.'

The friends started to speak different languages,
I know, it's an extraordinary thing to say,
But the Holy Spirit had really come,
So they sat down to pray.

Kieran Bailey (10)
St Mary's RC Junior School, Carshalton

The Nutty Auntie!

I have got an auntie
Who is a complete nutter,
All she drinks is tea
And all she eats is butter.

She has a crush on seven men,
She plays the electric guitar
And then she keeps a hen,
She is a complete nutter.

She walks straight through windows
And hates the colour pink.
She loves the colour blue,
Guess what else does she think?

She calls herself the world's greatest auntie,
(That's what she thinks),
Today she is on a boat trip,
I bet the ship sinks.

Not many people have aunties like this,
She is cool,
My auntie is an excellent cook,
She is rather a fool.

Joe Mendonça (10)
St Mary's RC Junior School, Carshalton

Aunties

Usually aunties wear cardigans
And they talk a lot too
And chat on the telephone
Also they have very old, old shoes

They are neat and tidy
They are very cuddly
They have a laugh
But they are not funny

My auntie is as young as a teenager
She has a silk jacket with zips
She has leopard skin trousers
She has lipstick for her lips

She has a picture of the Devil on her top
She's in every shop
She has a handbag
Also she has a rainbow top

I won't swap her
I like her very much
She is the best
And is top.

Niamh Goodwin (10)
St Mary's RC Junior School, Carshalton

My Auntie Anna

My auntie she's called Anna,
She is a little odd
She's not plump with long baggy skirts
That have buttons which have all popped off

She doesn't know how to sew
And hates herbal tea
Instead she's in a rock band
She plays the electric guitar
She drinks Coke and lemonade
She is a superstar

You know most aunties object to football
My auntie is not the same
She supports Leeds United
Alan Smith is her favourite player's name

My auntie is a stunning artist
She painted a fabulous portrait of me
She has travelled all over the world
Painting landscapes and the sea

My auntie is not the same as any other
Aunties I know
But I would never change her
Because she's the best auntie in the world!

Laura Rix (9)
St Mary's RC Junior School, Carshalton

My Vain Uncle

I have a vain uncle,
He's what uncles aren't supposed to be
And if you read this poem,
Then you will see.

He has blue hair
And it's quite long,
I wouldn't mind if
It was all gone.

He drives a small gold car
And it goes very slow,
He said 15 miles per hour
Is the fastest it will go.

He wears a bright pink shirt
And black and green shoes,
If you ask me,
I would prefer dirt.

He is crazy and weird,
But all in all he is a great guy,
But when I was young why
Didn't I choose someone else, oh why?

Adam Lowe
St Mary's RC Junior School, Carshalton

My Mum And I

My mum and I do everything together,
Everything together, no matter what the weather.
Last week we went shopping,
As we went home, we started hopping.
When we got home, we helped each other,
Then my dad came home with my brother.
We had dinner and talked a bit,
Then I got ready my football kit,
My mum's the best, she helps me a lot,
She helps me all the time no matter what,
Yesterday we went to the funfair,
We went on a ride that gave me a scare
But my mum was there.
We went on a carousel,
My mum and I went on a horse,
Then we went on the obstacle course.
Another day we went to the seaside,
It took ages to get there, it was such a long ride.
We sat on the sand watching the tide,
My mum and I do everything together,
Everything together, no matter what the weather.

Rachel Wright (10)
St Mary's RC Junior School, Carshalton

Dance Poem

D ance is an
A ctivity
N ice and relaxing, just like
C heerleading
E njoyable and
I nteresting and fun
N ew dances are learnt, come on it's
G reat.

Abigail Goulding (10)
St Mary's RC Junior School, Carshalton

A Witch's Poem

Let's make a building
A really gross one
We'll throw in nasty objects
Then stir them in a pot

Add: goo for cement
Brains for bricks
Put in the builder's hands
Don't forget the guts
Add: the blood from a hyena
The teeth from a tiger
The ears from an elephant
15 corpses from a pub

Let's make a building
A really gross one
We'll throw in nasty objects
Then stir them in a pot.

Cian Hodge
St Mary's RC Junior School, Carshalton

Alone In The Dark

Every night I am scared of the dark
All I see is shadow monsters
In the dark the killer will awake

When I need the toilet I don't pull the chain
Because if I do the killer will hear
Then send me to be caned

The killer is immortal some have tried
But all I know is they got taken away, then died

When I go to bed
All I can think of is losing my head
So I try to sleep
And I never hear a peep.

George Willes
St Mary's RC Junior School, Carshalton

Remember Me?

Remember me?
I was your friend,
the one you used to be with,
the one you used to whisper to
and always used to play with.

Remember me?
I used to shout,
I used to run around,
I used to jump up to the sky
and say 'Yippee!
oh I am very happy.'

Remember me?
I was at your house,
going to the park,
reading many books with you,
sometimes doing a dance.

Remember me?
It suddenly ended,
our friendship ripped apart,
you snarled at me and turned away
and it was over,
I turned away to cry.

Remember me?
Now I have new friends,
ones whom I can trust,
they're very kind and good to me
and we play late 'til dusk.

Laura Ireland (10)
St Mary's RC Junior School, Carshalton

Spooky Walk

I was lying tight in bed,
When suddenly I needed water,
In case I died of thirst,
I got out and risked slaughter.

I could wake up Mum and Dad,
But I decided not to
And leave them in peace
And do it before the cockerel went coo.

As I walked across the stairs
I thought eagerly that they would collapse
But then I knew it was all nonsense
And knew there were no traps.

But still what was that noise?
A monster under the stairs?
No, that was just the creaking of them
Of course there are no bears.

As I walked through the kitchen
Some clicks came from the ceiling
A ghost? No! No such things!
It was just the pipes retracting.

Now I've had my drink
And I'm back safe in bed
I feel so happy and relieved
No one got me and fled.

Alex Wantoch (10)
St Mary's RC Junior School, Carshalton

My Granny

When I first saw my gran
She looked rather mad,
But when I got to know her,
I was always very glad.

When I saw her earrings,
Eight inches wide,
I wasn't sure if they were real,
I doubt that they were real gold.

Once I'd seen her fingers,
I said, 'Oh my God!'
She asked me, 'What's the matter?'
I said, 'Your fingers are so long!'

When I saw her combing her hair,
I thought it was a wig,
I thought she'd be taller,
But she was only four feet big.

Elliot Chandler (10)
St Mary's RC Junior School, Carshalton

An Utterly Dotty Aunt

My aunt is not a normal aunt who will help you out or look after you,
Oh no, if I were you I'd be scared of her,
She wears platform boots, mini-skirts and crop tops
                                    in rainbow colours,
Her hair is permed and green but she still clips in those fluffy flowers,
She's not married, that's much too normal for her,
The thing she prefers is dating someone only once,
My aunt's house is as mad as her, none of the furniture matches,
The walls are either bright pink or yellow with big blue splotches,
Although, she's not always glam with mini-skirts and crop tops,
Occasionally she decides to wear long old lady skirts and jumpers!
Be afraid, *very afraid!*

Lucy Wynn (10)
St Mary's RC Junior School, Carshalton

Goldilocks

Goldilocks had a box full of pearls,
She tied them up in her golden curls,
Then went for a walk through the trees,
Tripped on a tree root and grazed her knees,
The beautiful pearls in her hair spread out everywhere,
Pixies in the grass who crawl
Saw the sparkling pearly jewels
The wicked pixies were dreadful thieves
They wrapped the pearls in bright green leaves
The little pixies flew away with the pearls
They hoped to play, the pixies realised they had been bad,
Quickly back they came with pearls,
To the little girl with the curls.

Nicola Whitehorn (11)
Stepgates Community School

Snow White

She was an angel who came from above,
She has pale white skin like a dove,
Her heart was a piece of gold,
Such a shame the queen is old,
The queen is always second best,
Snow White always won because of her dress,
Every time she sings to the well,
Her voice echoes and shakes the bell,
Her handsome prince saves her one day,
On a cruise they sailed away,
To a beautiful land of flowers,
Where they canoodled for hours and hours.

Georgina Smailes (11)
Stepgates Community School

Money!

Michael Morebucks is staggeringly wealthy,
Enormously fat (and not very healthy),
But a stingier man you could not wish to meet,
He would snigger at those who had nothing to eat,
But then one day he had no money,
He didn't find it a tiny bit funny,
His clothes got ruined and were all dirty,
He got tempted with a loan from Uncle Berty.
It wasn't very much,
He tried not to touch,
But he needed some food,
He tried not to be rude,
He snatched the dosh,
He missed being posh,
He ran to the shop
And got a new top,
He brought lots of snacks,
He got five packs of Tic-Tacs,
He shoved it down all in one,
Now this was his idea of fun,
All of a sudden he felt all funny,
He suddenly thought
Could he be better without his money?

Jae Eldridge (10)
Stepgates Community School

Mrs Jacob

Mrs Jacob is a Year 6 teacher
And this is her best feature
She is good at French, she speaks the lingo
On Saturday nights she plays bingo
She teaches Spanish at Manuel's school
The pupils think she is really cool
Her husband is a policeman
He drives a huge police van.

Dean Manyonga (11)
Stepgates Community School

Superhero Nero

The boring old wrinkly Nero,
Tried to be a superhero,
Down his throat went plates of Brussels,
But didn't get a single muscle,
On the TV he saw Popeye,
His favourite programme caught his eye,
A light bulb shone as he got ideas,
Spinach for lunch washed down with beers,
Every time he ate a sprout,
Instead of a hero he was a trout,
He knew he couldn't be a hero
And that's the end of great old Nero.

Samsun Gunaydin (11)
Stepgates Community School

William Why

William Why a brilliant kid,
Asked the same question whatever he did,
'Why are clouds white and in blue sky?'
William asked, 'I wonder why?
Why are polar bears so lovely and white?
William asked, 'Why are they so light?
'Why are monkeys so funny and cheeky?'
William asked, 'Why are they so sneaky?
Why are elephants so big and grey?'
That is what he will always say.
'Why do people have funny faces?
Why do people live in different places?'

Terri Gunner (11)
Stepgates Community School

School!

If you can go into assembly
And sit on a cold, bottom-numbing floor
If you can keep your hand up
And not even get asked one single question
If you can get all of your own PE kit back
Into your bag on time
If you can eat a horrible, cold, mouldy
And sickly-looking dinner without being sick
If you can do your best piece of work
And stay calm when someone copies it
If you can give a lifetime bully a second chance
Then you're a bigger person than I'll ever be!

Harriet Evans (11)
Stepgates Community School

The Hulk

When the Hulk is angry he is very green,
He is the biggest man you've ever seen.
When the Hulk rips his clothes,
He takes up a ginormous pose.
He'll lift up anything, he's almighty strong,
He loves music, he'll sing you a song.
The Hulk's muscles are bigger than yours,
He'll blow you away with terrifying roars.
The Hulk is very athletic,
If he chases you he'll make you pathetic.
So this is a warning to you all,
Don't make the Hulk lose his cool.

Jordan Arnold (11)
Stepgates Community School

The Elegy Of The Tomatoes

I can't bear it,
That sharp knife going through the head,
Every day we are served
On a thin piece of bread.

My family is dead,
I am very, very sad,
They got chopped up,
Humans are very, very bad.

I will be dead,
They will chop off my arms and legs,
They will pick me up
And hang me above the boiling water with pegs.

I have one friend who is a human,
His name is Bob,
He will protect me,
He does a great job.

Edward Butler (10)
The Royal Kent School

The Elegy Of Potatoes

I hate potatoes
I peel the skin
I savagely slice them
I always win
I mash potatoes
I turn them to pies
I crumble them up
I turn them to fries

I eat potatoes
I boil the skin
I put them in hot water
I throw them in the bin.

Joe Marchant (10)
The Royal Kent School

A Snowy Night

As
 A
  Man
   Walks
    Through
    The
     Forest
     The
      Trees
       Sleepwalk
      In
       The
       Breeze
      And
       Snow
        Trickling
        Down

His back, he sees in the opening
A light, a light brighter than any other light,
It was his home,
He stopped and imagined the blazing fire that awaited him,
Meanwhile the moonlight shining like a diamond in the night sky
Leads the route home.

Pierre Regnault (10)
The Royal Kent School

The Orange

On the table I sit crushed up just like soup,
My cousin is locked in a jar,
Marmalised and ready,
We were plucked from the family tree
Peeled and crushed with your teeth
Enjoyed by every piece.

Callum Shepherd (9)
The Royal Kent School

Fairy Land

Down my garden, at the very end,
Past the shed and round the bend.
Where the daisies and roses grow
And scattered pansies to and fro.

But if you look closer still,
You will find a pleasant thrill.
You'll see tiny footprints in the mud
And hear a tiny thud, thud, thud.

Follow where the footprints go,
But don't you run, no take it slow.
Keep following them to Fairy Land,
Were fairies wear their dresses, grand.

Where fairies ride about on frogs
And keep ladybirds as if they were dogs.
Where they sleep in a toadstool house,
In which they live with a little white mouse.

Their wings are big, their faces small,
They haven't any shoes at all.
Their clothes are made from the petals of flowers
And trees to them are great big towers.

Are you amazed at what you've seen?
And all the fairy places you've been?
But now it's time to say goodbye,
But hold your breath and take your time.
Back past the bend and round the shed,
But please come again to see your fairy friends.

Grace Kennard (10)
The Royal Kent School

Fingers -Haiku

Fingers are tasty
Crunchy and tempting, you can't
Resist the flavour.

Matthew Langdon (10)
The Royal Kent School

Carrots

You kill carrots a lot
You chop off lots of heads
Then crunch us in Christmas dinner
And soak us in gravy beds

Then you have us crunched
Strip us of our skins
You chop off our bums
Throw the rest into bins

You're really gruesome
Stop having us sliced
Stomp us into mash
You're getting me diced

You are really evil
Cutting off our hair
You are really evil
Then you strip us bare

So farewell
I must die
I am afraid to say
Goodbye . . .

Christopher Styan (9)
The Royal Kent School

The Lady Of Oxshott

As she raced in her limo
And smartened up her pink bow,
The tears down her face began to flow,
She gave her nose a great big blow.
The lady of Oxshott
She was feeling rather blue
She thought she had the flu, *atchoo!*
But how did she get it?
She did not have a clue!
The lady of Oxshott.

Katrina Hughes (9)
The Royal Kent School

The Lady Of Oxshott

There she goes in her new sports car, driving off,
She's going far
She loves her mansion that's painted pink
She's going to buy that beautiful mink
The lady of Oxshott

Off she goes in her Mercedes Benz
She's got lots of money to spend, spend

At 12 o'clock she decides to stop
To have some lunch before she flops
The lady of Oxshott

At 2.30
She's feeling perky
To tackle the shops this time
She's feeling quite fine
The lady of Oxshott.

Emily Godfrey (9)
The Royal Kent School

Daffodils

There they sway in the field of gold,
Whistling and humming over the breeze,
That magical feel of gleaming satin
And that taste of sweet lemon sauce and honey.

The smell of strong, sweet perfume,
Seeing a stampede of singing angels,
As you walk through them,
They sway against your uncovered legs.

Seeing them I feel warm and happy,
Even when I leave the fields,
I still have that magical feeling,
That feeling of bright daffodils.

Sian Gray (10)
The Royal Kent School

A Day In The Life Of School

It's Monday morning,
I'm half asleep,
I fall out of my bed,
To go and brush my teeth.

I plod down the stairs,
Yawning as I go,
Then I eat my breakfast,
I eat it nice and slow.

I climb up the stairs,
I get dressed nice and fast,
I jump into the car,
Finally, at last!

In school, we learn,
Science, maths and art,
Lots of pupils buzzing with ideas,
In other words they're smart.

Time to go home,
It's the end of the day,
But when we come back tomorrow,
We will be back to *play!*

Fiona Horrod (10)
The Royal Kent School

Daffodils

I can feel smooth silk
I can see a golden ball shining in the sun
I feel happy and jolly inside
I can hear angels singing in the breeze
They taste like soft butter and honey
They smell like lemon sherbet
Daffodils make me feel like the happiest girl on Earth.

Danielle Wilson (10)
The Royal Kent School

The Elegy Of The Tomatoes

The tomatoes are out to get you,
Because you threw them at the stage,
They splattered at the wall,
And some of them were at a very young age.

You fry them and cook them,
One of them is dead,
You dropped him into salad
And sliced right through his head.

I can't stand it any longer,
My friends are being killed,
You put them in the freezer
And now they're getting chilled.

Natalie Hooper (10)
The Royal Kent School

Daffodils

The taste of sour lemon and sweet butter
Swishing and swaying in the wind
A crustling and rustling sound
Watching daffodils makes me feel happy
They match with the sky
Like bright golden stars shimmering
Shining in the sun
So soft, but yet so silky
Smell like honey
They whistle in the wind
And make me cheerful.

Eman Omer (9)
The Royal Kent School

Monstrous Snowmen

I built a snowman 10 feet tall,
But I could not reach it, cos I was so small,
I tried to screw up paper for his eyes,
So I nicked a few of my dad's ties,
When I used a ladder, I failed,
Next time I did it, I got nailed.
I managed to put on one eye,
But there was a storm and it flew into the sky.
I went on the roof and had a Coke,
But when I jumped down the snowman broke.
I was upset cos I got so near,
Oh well, there's always next year.

Jack Montague (10)
The Royal Kent School

Cauliflower

'I hate cauliflower,'
Said Rachel one evening tea,
But what she didn't know
Cauliflowers hear and see.

'I once liked you,' said the cauliflower,
'But you boiled me twice.
I was so, so hot
I didn't have much choice.

You cut me up
You bit off my head
I felt very ill until . . .
I found a comfy bed.'

Rachel Bradford (9)
The Royal Kent School

Autumn

In autumn when the trees are bare
And no longer have any leaves to spare
They drop conkers for us to roast
And we can jump in all the leaves
The dark red, browns, yellows and greens,
The hedgehog curls into his spiky little ball
And the slugs and snails slowly crawl,
The leaves are falling
Nature is crawling,
All on an autumn day.

Tjasha Stroud (10)
The Royal Kent School

Autumn Leaves

The autumn leaves sway in the breeze,
They look so pretty when they freeze,
The wonderful colours gold, brown and green
And the sunshine peering through with a golden beam.

Josh Corrigan (10)
The Royal Kent School

Tiger

Eyes burn like fire,
More than my desire,
Its heart pounds like a hammer,
Boom, boom, boom!
On the prowl,
More orange than fire,
Killing gazelles unaware.

Daniel Goudie (10)
Woodside Junior School

Family Sonnet

Let me tell you about my family
We live in Croydon, Surrey
There's Mum, there's Dad, there's Sophie and me
We all like eating curry
My mum can run very far
She ran the marathon you know
My dad's got a brand new car
But he drives it ever so slow
My sister's got a rabbit for a pet
It's very small and cute
I can play the clarinet
And also the flute
That is all I have to say
I'll tell you more another day.

Naomi Harrison (10)
Woodside Junior School

EastEnders

EastEnders is the one place to be,
Monday, Tuesday, Thursday and Friday for me.
Albert Square is so cool,
I wish we could watch it at school.
Kat and Alfie live on top of the pub
And they are also in love.
All the markets lined up in a row,
Lots of people are working except Big Mo.
Dirty Den is here again
And Andy is beating up lots of men,
The Watts family are back on top
And in charge of the launderette is holy Dot.

Shenaid Tapper (10)
Woodside Junior School

Nature

Nature is beautiful,
I wish there was a waterfall,
There's trees with leaves,
Flowers with the power to shine,
Could all this be mine?

Grass that grows fast,
With ants that creep and crawl,
Butterflies fly gently through the air,
While the birds and the bees live in the trees,
Staring at nature can bring you to your knees.

Jodie Micallef (9)
Woodside Junior School

The Waves Hit The Shore

The waves hit the shore,
But what do they do it for?
Are they angry? Are they sad?
Are they feeling kind of bad?
I'll always ask the question,
'Why do waves hit the shore?'

William Dunne
Woodside Junior School

Art

Art is brilliant and artistic
And I think it's so realistic
It's unavoidable
And also enjoyable
But when my dad saw
The state of me
He went ballistic!

Bakhitah Bundu-Kamara (10)
Woodside Junior School

My First Strawberry

When I was three,
I had my first strawberry,
It was my mum who gave it to me,
She had hand-picked it,
It was red,
It was sweet,
It was juicy,
But most of all it was full of love.

Sheldon Kyme (9)
Woodside Junior School

Graffiti

Graffiti, graffiti why are you here?
I really don't like you, you're everywhere!
Please don't show up
Please go away
Take your scribble and your spray
How would you like it if I scribbled on your wall?
You're thick and stupid and don't care at all.

Amy Lackenby (8)
Woodside Junior School

The Man Who Hurt His Nose

There was a man from Highbury,
He needed to go to the library,
Having a bad day,
He had a large bill to pay,
But he got his nose stuck in a book on bribery.

Geoffrey Whitby (10)
Woodside Junior School

Living In Jamaica

When I woke up in the morning
I heard singing birds outside
Flying to the top of the tree
The sky is blue
The sun is bright
Outside is warm
The grass is green and the tree trunk is long
Sometimes I just sit down and dream
My grandma and grandfather sometimes ask me to help them
With the beautiful garden
Because they want me to help plant new flowers.

Tajay Ashmeade (10)
Woodside Junior School

My Hamster

When my hamster died,
It was really sad,
When I found out, I cried.
Now I feel really bad,
If only it wasn't so hot,
He wouldn't have died,
But I still love him a lot!

Jamie Lowe (9)
Woodside Junior School

My Brother Daniel

Have you ever met my brother Daniel?
If my brother doesn't get his own way
He will scream the house down,
But you can't get enough of him,
He's funny,
He's cute and cuddly.

Kelly Henry (9)
Woodside Junior School

Mum's Cool Car!

Mum's cool car!
The new Ford Star,
The engine smells of egg!
It's comfy like a bed,
It's a convertible! A red one!
It can go at top speed,
My mates just love it indeed.

Mum's cool car!
The new Ford Star,
It's not at all bumpy,
When the music is on
It turns all funky!
It's boring when it's wet,
We can't have the roof down,
But still I love my mum and her car!

Lauren Carr (9)
Woodside Junior School

Funny Family

My family is very, very funny
And I wish they could behave,
In front of my friends
They behave like kids (sometimes anyway),
But in front of my grandma
They behave like adults, finally.

My mother's OK!
But sometimes my dad is really silly!
I wonder why?
I ask God seriously,
I really wonder why?

Janaki Srikanthan (9)
Woodside Junior School

Just One More Go!

I'm going to the funfair,
With Mum, Dad and Sis,
There's 10 pound in my pocket,
There's no prize I'm gonna miss.

I'm going to the funfair,
What a place to be,
Candyfloss and roller coasters,
People going, 'Wheee!'

I'm going to the funfair,
I'm on the coconut shy,
I compete against my sister,
Aw! It's a tie.

I'm going to the funfair,
I want another try,
I'm spending all my money,
On the coconut shy!

I'm going to the funfair,
'Just one more go!'
It cost two pound,
I'm not spending slow!

I'm going home from the funfair,
I spent all my money,
Trying to hit coconuts,
It wasn't very funny!

Charlotte Devenish (9)
Woodside Junior School

The Talking Pet

My pet isn't normal,
She talks and does my homework,
I don't!
Instead I stuff my mouth with popcorn
And play computer games,
When my mum comes in,
I say, 'Bettie why are you chewing my homework again?'
I love my pet rabbit,
I give her extra food to do my homework,
That's the charge for it!

Seraish Edwards (9)
Woodside Junior School

Seaside

It was a warm day when I went to the seaside
I went for a swim and saw lots of fish
I came back out and was walking on wet stones and soggy sand
I started to make a sandcastle with my sister
And put shells on the top
And I went home with my family.

Jessica Kidd
Woodside Junior School

Friends

Leanne is my best friend
The friend to end all friends
But even when we broke up
We settled it in the end
Now we are friends again
Friends again
I wouldn't break up again.

Jodie McQuade (9)
Woodside Junior School

I'm Happy To Be Alive

I'm happy to be alive today,
I'm happy to be alive,
I'm nice, not horrible,
I'm pretty, not ugly,
I'm happy to be alive.
My mum is nice,
She makes me breakfast,
She's the one who brought me into the world,
She loves me, doesn't hate me,
I'm happy to be alive.

Nikki Mikellides (8)
Woodside Junior School

Hamsters

My hamster's gentle fur,
The touch of his tickling feet,
His pink little nose,
His sharp pointed teeth,
His small stick-up ears,
His long winding whiskers.

Eden Reeves Lamb
Woodside Junior School

Sun, Oh Sun

Sun, oh sun are you lighter than a bull?
Are you a giant star or a super star?
I wish I was clever and understood.

Sun, oh sun are you bigger than Earth?
Are you a giant parent or Superman?
I wish I was clever and understood.

Daniel Clayton (8)
Woodside Junior School

Cats And Dogs

Cats
A cat's life is the best there could be,
To get in a house you don't need a key,
A cat's life is lazy and rude,
They just sit there waiting for food,
A cat's life is never really silly,
I don't have a cat but if I did I'd call it Billy!

Dogs
A dog's life is the best there could be,
Except when you have to chase a cat up a tree,
A dog's life is not lazy but fair,
Because when they need food it is always there.

A dog's life is playful and fun
I had a race with a dog - obviously he won!

Charley Pilbro
Woodside Junior School

My Busted Hotel

My Busted hotel
Is rich and posh
My Busted hotel
Has lots of dosh

My Busted hotel
Has Charlie, Matt and James
My Busted hotel
I put them in frames

My Busted hotel
Has all my mates
And Charlie, Matt and James
Are on the gates.

Crystal Medcalf
Woodside Junior School

My Best Friend Poem

Jack is my friend,
He's not just a friend,
He's a funny friend.

His brother is a devil,
He's not just a devil,
He's a crazy friend.

Miley is my friend,
He's not just a friend,
He's a *strong* friend!

Daniel is my friend,
He's not just a friend,
He's a funny friend.

But I have a *big* friend,
You know who?
My mates and my family.

Melad Ali
Woodside Junior School

My Best Holiday

My best holiday is Spain
They have lovely pasta
But it tastes ever so plain!

My best holiday is France
Because the people there
Like to dance!

No, but my best holiday is Jamaica
Because you can always
Visit the baker!

Sachadena Walker (9)
Woodside Junior School

All About My Pets

I've got a cat who sits on my mat.
I've got a dog who sits on my log.
I've got rabbits that have some habits.
I've got a parrot who eats my carrots.
I've got a guinea pig that did a really big dig.
I've got a mouse who lives in my house.
I've got a lion who likes to iron.
I've got a bird who says rude words.
I've got a fly who always applies.
I've got a horse that likes doing a racing course.
I've got a fish who likes to go on a dish.
I've got a pig that likes to do a jig.

Molly Algar
Woodside Junior School

Funfair

At the funfair
I go on a ride,
A very fast ride,
It starts lowly,
Boring!
It gets faster and faster,
Until I feel sick,
I'm glad the ride's over,
I really need the toilet - quick!

William Howells (8)
Woodside Junior School

Oh Brother

Oh brother, oh brother, take me to school
Oh brother, oh brother, I'll get to the pool
Oh brother, oh brother, how will you do?
Oh brother, oh brother, tie my shoe?

Asim Qureshi (8)
Woodside Junior School

Questions

Oh sun, oh sun are you lighter than a bulb?
Are you a giant star or a super star?
Oh sun please tell me what you are.

Oh moon, oh moon are you shinier than frozen ice?
Are you really made from cheese?
Oh moon please tell me what you are.

Oh Jupiter, oh Jupiter are you really the biggest planet in the system?
Do you really need your rings?
Oh Jupiter please tell me what you are.

Michael Vernon (9)
Woodside Junior School

Little Creatures

A pixie so small
A pixie so tall
A fairy so young
A fairy so glum
An imp so mystical
An imp so magical
A gnome so big
A gnome like a pig.

Leah Anderson (9)
Woodside Junior School

SATs

S itting on the chair in silence
A nxiously waiting for the test paper
T he table seems lonely
S itting on the chair in silence.

Sheridan Wyllie
Woodside Junior School

Numbers

7
8
9
10
Those numbers are in my head again
37
38
39
40
That bully is being naughty
107
108
109
110
I went on holiday then
137
138
139
140
Everything is getting sorted.

Sophie Parker (10)
Woodside Junior School

Smoking

Why don't you stop, Grandad?
You said you would stop smoking.
You're always giving me headaches,
You said you would stop just for me.
Please, please stop, I'm scared,
I don't want you to be unwell,
Why don't you stop, Grandad?

Rianna Louis (9)
Woodside Junior School